WOMEN OF DESTINY

WOMEN OF DESTINY

Women in the Old Testament

Lucy Fuchs, PhD
Saint Leo College

ALBA·HOUSE   alba house   NEW·YORK
SOCIETY OF ST. PAUL, 2187 VICTORY BLVD., STATEN ISLAND, NEW YORK 10314

ST PAULS

Library of Congress Cataloging-in-Publication Data

Fuchs, Lucy.
    Women of destiny: women in the Old Testament / Lucy Fuchs.
        p.   cm.
    Includes bibliographical references.
    ISBN 0-8189-0863-7
    1. Women in the Bible.   2. Bible. O.T. — Criticism,
Interpretation, etc.   I. Title.
BS575.F83   1999
221.9'22'082 — dc21   99-13186
    [B]   CIP

Produced and designed in the United States of America by the
Fathers and Brothers of the Society of St. Paul,
2187 Victory Boulevard, Staten Island, New York 10314,
as part of their communications apostolate.

ISBN: 0-8189-0863-7

Printing Information:

Current Printing - first digit   1   2   3   4   5   6   7   8   9   10

Year of Current Printing - first year shown

2000   2001   2002   2003   2004   2005   2006   2007   2008   2009

Table of Contents

Introduction

THE WOMEN OF THE OLD TESTAMENT ARE QUITE DIFFERENT from the women in the New Testament. At first glance they attract us less. In the New Testament, Martha and Mary at Bethany with their ministrations to Jesus, Mary Magdalen with her loving sorrow, Mary, Jesus' own mother, are all admirable women. They are gentle, loving, and wise individuals who served the needs of others.

In the Old Testament we find Judith who cuts off Holofernes' head, Jael who drives a tent peg through Sisera's head, and Deborah who counsels war. We also find the envious Miriam, the murderous Jezebel, the conniving Rebecca. These are women of a sterner stuff. Yet their stories show them to be real women, women who took on life as it was presented to them and played dramatically their roles in life.

In every case their roles were larger than they were, for all of them were part of the first act, called the Old Testament, of the great drama of the redemption. These women speak to us down through the centuries. They may be models of behavior, or they may be misfits, or they may simply be mothers of famous men, but they all are Women of Destiny.

This book is dedicated to my elementary school teachers, the

Sisters of the Precious Blood, great women all, who taught me not only the joys of reading books, but of reading The Book.

Thank you.

BEGINNING WITH THE BEGINNING

Eve

THIS IS THE STORY OF THE BEGINNING OF WOMANKIND. MAN is alone among the other creatures that God has made. He is intelligent and powerful and close to God but he is lonely. He needs someone else. God himself notices the deficiency: "It is not good for man to be alone."

Man needs someone like him, yet not like him, someone of equal status, but different. The animals are less than he is and he knows it and God is far far above him and he knows that too. So God decides to create a suitable partner for Adam. To do this he does something that he does in the creation of no other creature. He takes a part of his creature Adam to make this second human. He puts Adam to sleep, the story tells us, and takes one of his ribs to form a woman. This part of the story emphasizes that man and woman are part of the same flesh; they are meant to be two in one flesh.

What a beautiful story this is. Persons familiar with reading Genesis will recognize that this story comes from the second story of creation in the Bible, the "J," Yahwistic account. In the first chapter of Genesis we have another story of creation, the "P," or

Priestly account, in which we are told simply, "Then God said,
'Let us make man in our image, after our likeness; and let them
have dominion over the fish of the sea, and over the birds of the
air, and over the cattle, and over the earth, and over every creep-
ing thing that creeps upon the earth.' So God created man in his
own image, in the image of God he created him; male and female
he created them."

Yet in both these traditions we find the same basic truth:
Woman was created alongside man to be a companion to him. Men
and women were meant to be together. They needed each other at
the very beginning of the world and they still each other.

Both of these stories embody theological truths rather than
historical truths. No one was present at the creation. No one was
there with a reporter's notebook taking down God's actions nor
questioning him for his reasons, such as: "Now, Sir, just why did
you create woman?"

The theological truths are simply that all things have their
origin in God, that man and woman are both and equally creations
of God, that they are much more alike than they are different.

Further, there are strong sexual elements in the story of creation. All the living things that God created are endowed with the
ability to propagate themselves, especially through sexual behavior. God saw that it was good. The attraction between the male and
the female is a strong attraction and a very good one. That is the
way life, given by God, is to be carried on. God loves the creatures
of his hands.

We might wonder what Eve looked like. At least to Adam,
she was beautiful. He was very pleased to meet her and share his
life with her. He exclaimed, "This at last is bone from my bones,
and flesh from my flesh."

Human beings are God's special creatures, both male and
female. He made both and wanted and needed them both. There

is no question of one being a lesser creature; they are partners. One wonders how some later medieval scholars who surely loved and meditated the Scriptures, could have termed women misbegotten men. How strange indeed.

Women have often been treated as second-class in many cultures through much of history, and ancient writings reflect this. This story from the Bible, however, was different. Here Eve was created to be with man, not to be excluded. That first man, Adam, needed her and she needed him. Together they were to be fruitful and multiply.

Although this was surely meant in the sense of reproduction, of having and nurturing children and building the human race, there is another equally important meaning. Together man and woman are most fruitful. When they work together they accomplish a great deal. When they work at odds with one another, much good that could be accomplished is left undone. There is no need to put woman above man, as though as God went about the work of creation, he got better at it, but because woman was created second, she is not secondary. After all, God created the animals before he created man.

What this story seems to demonstrate is that man and woman are meant to be together, to work together in mutual respect, and simply to love each other.

Discussion:

1. Why do you suppose the author used the idea of God's taking a rib from Adam in order to create Eve? What significance, if any, do you see in that? Why did he not use more of the dust of the earth?
2. What subtle differences do you see in the creation stories of

men and women in Chapter 1 and in Chapter 2 of Genesis? Which elements of creation does each emphasize?

3. Visualize the response of Adam when he first sees Eve? How do you think Eve viewed him?

THAT DAY IN THE GARDEN

The Fall of Woman

ONE DAY EVE WALKED IN THE BEAUTIFUL GARDEN THAT God had created for her and Adam. There in the garden a snake, the most cunning of all the creatures so the story goes, lay waiting. He spoke to Eve and in his cunning and her naivete convinced her that if she ate the fruit of the tree of knowledge of good and evil, she would become like God. She ate, she gave to Adam and he ate likewise, and thus fell the human race.

It would be more accurate, perhaps, to say thus fell woman. Because ever since that fateful day in the garden the argument can be made that women have borne the brunt of the fall.

Scripture scholars assure us that this is all a myth, that it is an attempt to explain the world as it is, full of sorrows and woes, including the biggest sorrow of all, death. It portrays no historical truth. There were no on-the-spot written accounts to this momentous event in the garden. Nor was there a statement issued by God himself about something called original sin. The theological explanation came much much later.

The snake is not in this story associated with Satan; that interpretation also came later. The serpent was a common figure in fertility cults and in this story it was through the serpent that Adam and Eve realized that they were naked and needed to cover themselves. Up to this time they were innocent, so to speak.

As ancient as this story and its interpretations are, the world today is still influenced by it.

Because of this story, women for centuries were to consider themselves the cause of sin. This was reinforced by some of the most noted of Catholic theologians. Woman was the temptress; she it was who could lead, with a single glance of her eye, a holy man down the path of perdition. This would be laughable if it weren't so sad because it had the most lamentable effects on women.

Very commonly throughout history, women have been oppressed. Their chief goal in life, it seemed, was to give birth to children, but they often suffered great pain in childbirth. Further, women were strongly attracted to men, yet they were often subjected to the whims of men who treated them as nothing more than personal slaves.

However, men have suffered too. A large proportion of men through the centuries have been engaged in agriculture, and agriculture has not usually been a simple task. Tilling the soil was and is hard and frequently there is little to show for it, except thorns and thistles. But other work is often painful and difficult too. One need only think of the monotonous and long hours of work men have had to endure in factories and mines.

Ultimately, both man and woman, after all the turmoil and torments of life, succumb to death. No one could conquer death itself.

Surely, the storytellers thought, this could not be the way a loving God wanted the world to be. Surely, something must have happened to make things this way. And so the story unfolded.

It is a very good story. Yet it must be remembered that it is simply that, a story. It explains what is happening in the world without setting a blueprint for what should be.

It is interesting to note that when medications were invented in the nineteenth century that made childbirth less painful, some physicians and some theologians argued against using them on the consideration that women were supposed to suffer in childbirth, that they could gain redemption in no other way. It is strange that there is no evidence of any such arguments when farm machinery was invented that removed so much of the sweat of the brow from farm labor. (Large tractors today even have air-conditioning and music.)

It is unfortunate that even serious-minded men have used this story to continue the oppression of women. What is even more unfortunate is the effect it has had on women themselves. Some women dislike being women; they have swallowed whole the idea that they are less worthy creatures. Others have accepted the idea that women are less capable. As a result, they have not used their talents to their full ability, considering that they are really not very good. It seems that, as psychological studies have shown, many women have a very low self-concept. Such a low self-concept keeps women from achieving what they might well achieve. It also per-mits them to accept a second-class condition of life.

What then can we do with this story today? As the ancients used this story to explain the world as they saw it, we too can see it as explaining a fallen world. The effects are surely here with us. But rather than seeing woman being punished for leading Adam astray, we can see the full effects of that early sin for all of the hu-man race. The oppression of women is truly an effect of sin; it is not intended by a loving God. It will take that message a long time to sink in.

Discussion:

1. How do you feel when you read this story? Does it inspire you, sadden you, anger you, or have another effect on you?
2. Why do you think that the punishment of Eve has been stressed throughout the centuries, but not the punishment of Adam?
3. Do you think that many men, like Adam, still blame women for the ills of the world? Do women blame men for the ills of the world?

Genesis 11:29-12:20

THE WOMAN WHO WAS CHILDLESS

Sarai

T HE FIRST TIME WE MEET SARAI WE ARE TOLD SIMPLY THAT Abram was married to her and that she was barren, having no child.

In those days that said already a great deal about a woman. To have a child was a woman's destiny. Although, as we have seen, the suffering that went with childbirth was severe and apparently a direct result of a woman's sin, childbirth was what all women wanted. Without children women were nobodies, sad creatures with no claim to a full life on earth, nor would they be remembered after their deaths. How could they be, with no descendants to live on?

We see that Abram and Sarai were already old. We have no idea what Sarai's deepest thoughts were, nor do we have any idea of how resigned she may have been by the time Abram met his God.

God told him to go to another land. Here is the beginning of the Jewish people. Abram, whose name would eventually be changed to Abraham, was called to be the father of a great nation. He believed his God, but he must have wondered how. To be a father meant that there must be a mother and Sarai's fruitful years were already past.

Then, before he could even begin to set up a new nation, famine struck. Abram went to Egypt to escape the famine. As he went to Egypt he was worried.

His wife Sarai, in spite of her age, was apparently still very beautiful. Abram was concerned that when the Egyptians saw her, they would want her, and so kill him to take her. He told Sarai to say that she was his sister. In that way he would be well-treated because of her. Abram here was much more concerned about himself than he was about his wife Sarai. He was quite willing to compromise her. After all, he might have said to himself, she was sterile.

Does this sound harsh to us? If so, it was a harsh world for women in those days, as it still is for many women. It was understood that a woman was a man's property, including and especially her body. If a husband chose to put his wife's body at another man's disposal, he had that right.

What Abram predicted would happen did happen. The Egyptians were immediately attracted to Sarai and reported to the Pharaoh of her beauty. Pharaoh took her into his palace and she became one of his wives. Abram was well treated by the Pharaoh for this gift of his "sister." He was rewarded with flocks and oxen and slaves. We can only wonder about Sarai's life in the palace and how she felt about Abram during this time.

But things did not go well in the palace. God, it seemed, sent down plagues and other disasters, apparently showing that he did not approve of what was going on.

Just who told Pharaoh the truth, we do not know. Perhaps the Pharaoh realized one day that all his tribulations began at about the same time that he brought Sarai in. He may have called her and questioned her. Perhaps it was she who revealed the truth. In any case, the Pharaoh now called Abram and gave him back his wife, told him to take her and all the gifts he had received so far, and go.

In many ways this is a terrible story, certainly not a very edifying one for the man who was chosen to be the father of a great nation, a nation into which God would eventually send his own Son.

Sarai comes across sadly here. It was commonly thought that the failure to give birth was a woman's fault. No one knew about low sperm count or any of the other conditions which can originate in the male and cause sterility. Childlessness was the woman's fault, even her moral fault. Children were gifts from God and if God chose not to give a child, it was surely because somehow or other, the woman was not worthy.

Sarai must have surely been conscious of the stigma she carried about her.

Later when she lived with the Pharaoh and because of her, he was visited with plagues, she must have felt doubly tainted. Some may interpret this story as showing divine disapproval on a man, the Pharaoh, taking another man's wife, even unknowingly. The Hebrew mind could conceive of that kind of divine action. Yet Pharaoh acted out of ignorance and if anyone should be punished it should have been Abram. He, however, came out ahead in this story; at least he was blessed with many material things at a time when his countrymen were suffering starvation.

But Sarai is the tainted one. How many times did Abram tell her of God's message to him, how he would be the father of a mighty nation. And how often she would again feel that she failed him, not only him but God himself.

As we read this story, we feel sympathy for Sarai. Later we will see that she had her faults too, but here at least let us spare her some compassion. She suffered what all women do who are made to feel that only having children is what their lives are all about, that somehow they contaminate others, that somehow they are not worthy creatures in themselves. In other words, she suffered from what has for centuries been the lot of womankind.

Discussion:

1. How do you picture Sarai, the older but still very beautiful woman? What kind of relationship did she have with her husband?
2. Can you think of any way of justifying Abram's behavior in Egypt?
3. What can women today learn from the behavior of Sarai, which seems to be mostly simply acceptance of her lot in life?

WOMB ENVY

Sarai and Hagar

GOD TOLD ABRAHAM HE WOULD BE THE FATHER OF A GREAT nation. He made a solemn promise to Abraham, a covenant, he gave him his divine word.

Abraham never doubted, but he surely wondered. His wife Sarai was apparently totally barren, unable to give him a son. How was he to have so many descendants, as numerous as the stars of heaven?

He went to sleep at night wondering and he woke in the morning wondering. Many times he asked Sarai what she thought.

She thought about it all the time too. She had only one practical solution. She would give Abraham her slave girl as a surrogate wife. Maybe she could have a child by him. It was not unusual, in the customs of the times, for a man to have a child by his wife's slave and that child to be considered her child, as it surely was his.

It must have been with great misgiving that she gave Hagar to her husband and then she must have watched day by day to see if indeed Hagar would be blessed with a child.

It wasn't long before Sarai could see that Hagar was pregnant and very happily pregnant, proudly pregnant. As all women wanted to give birth to children, this young Hagar (for surely she must have been quite young compared to Sarai) must have felt very honored. She was going to give birth to the great man's child, something even his wife had not been able to do. Somehow she, although a slave, must be a bit more worthy. She may even have considered herself more desirable to Abraham than Sarai was, in spite of Sarai's great beauty.

Hagar strutted around the house, proudly showing her swollen stomach. And when Sarai ordered her to do the household tasks that were always her lot, she showed her reluctance and took advantage of her condition. She, the woman pregnant by Abraham, being ordered by Sarai, the old useless wife — how could she? And she showed her disdain for Sarai.

Sarai rued the day she gave Hagar to her husband. She hated the way Hagar was acting, but if she was honest with herself, she knew that she was mostly envious. Why should this slave girl be given the privilege that she, the legitimate wife, was denied? She complained to Abraham.

He must have been irritated when she came to him. Not only did he have to oversee all the flocks and herds and servants of his own, but now these two women were squabbling. After all, it had been Sarai's idea for him to bed Hagar. Now she had only herself to blame.

Take care of it in your own way, he told her. And she did.

Sarai became exceedingly harsh with Hagar. Hagar soon learned that although she was bearing Abraham's child, she was not equal to being his wife. Sarai still ran the roost. And Abraham would allow Sarai to do as she wished.

As the days went by and Sarai's shrill voice and harsh commands and perhaps even physical abuse continued, Hagar felt she could take no more. She fled.

But she needed to be in the home of Sarai and Abraham. God

sent an angel to urge her to go back. Her son, although not the promised one, would still be an important son. She must go back and endure what she had to. God himself would look after her.

Hagar returned to the home of Sarai.

To us today, the whole story seems rather distasteful. The idea of Sarai's giving her slave girl to Abraham (and even of her having a slave girl whose person she can dispose of in that manner) does not edify us. Nor does Hagar's obvious overbearing manner. Nor do we admire the cruelty and spitefulness of Sarai. We cannot admire the behavior of these women, nor that of Abraham, who seems very passive. We must look beyond their behavior at the mores of the times and the lessons this story was meant to teach.

As we well know, both Sarai and Hagar saw their worth as women in their ability to have children. This explains much of the behavior of Sarai. She was so anxious to give her husband a child that she was willing to give him her slave girl. But then she could not cope with the consequences. Hagar's conduct, too, is easily explained. This was the first time she ever did anything better than her mistress. What an example of womb envy. To have a child was what mattered.

The message for us today is not so much the value of giving birth to children. Rather it focuses on God's call to each of us. Sarai and Hagar accepted the situation of their lives, as mistress and slave girl. Sarai suffered and reacted badly, but so did Hagar. And yet God wanted her to stay. Her son, conceived as he was through a mistaken idea, was still a worthwhile human being.

God can work with us in spite of mistakes and in spite of even wrong-headed behavior, and yes, in spite of even downright sin. God knows what he is doing. He is also much more tolerant than most people are. We are the ones to condemn others' behavior. We don't find God doing that in this story.

Discussion:

1. Are you appalled at Sarai's behavior in this story? What do you think of Abraham here? Do you see him as sort of a dreamer, who didn't quite have his finger on what was going on? (And yet we have seen him conniving.)
2. Is it true that no two women can live together in one house? If so, why?
3. What kind of women today could Hagar be compared to?

Genesis 19:15-26

THE SALT OF SORROW

Lot's Wife

WE KNOW VERY LITTLE ABOUT LOT'S WIFE. SHE HAS come down to us as the woman who, out of curiosity, looked back and was turned into a pillar of salt. And somehow or other, this was supposed to be a lesson about women's curiosity or perhaps her lack of obedience.

But let us look closer at the story. This was the age of Patriarchs, and men were the only important persons. Women had value, it seems, only according to their relationship with the men in their lives.

Here we have Lot's wife, whose name we do not even know, living with him in the very wicked city of Sodom. The favorite sin of the inhabitants was eventually given the name of their city. There were two daughters in this family, both young virgins. From what we know of this city, this family must truly have stood out from the rest.

Then visitors from God arrived. According to the ancient traditional law of hospitality, one was to sacrifice his own family for the sake of his visitors.

But here it seems to go too far. When the villagers of Sodom

17

called out to Lot that they wanted his visitors in order to abuse them (Could they really have been that bold and plain?) he offered them his young virgin daughters for their abuse.

What an incident!

We can imagine the situation. The crowd is outside the house shouting and banging on the doors and windows. Lot's wife is holding and trying to protect her daughters, their eyes wide with fear. And the two visitors are watching, something in their eyes showing a light not of this world.

Lot goes out to the crowd. They shout at him to release his guests. They are looking forward to an evening of sport with new and different persons.

Lot tries to appease them. He will not give them the heavenly visitors. His sense of hospitality is strong, but so is his belief that these visitors are angels from God and he dare not allow them to be abused. But he wants to quiet the crowd and get them to leave. Here is where he offers his daughters.

Inside, behind the walls of the house, the mother and daughters hear every word. The daughters must have been horrified. The mother must have felt outraged. How could she sacrifice her daughters? (It is interesting to note that although more than once God seems to ask of a man the sacrifice of his son, we know of no case where a woman was asked to sacrifice her daughter.) These women stood there, looking at each other and at the guests.

Then they heard the men of Sodom reject this offer. They threatened to take the guests by force and Lot along with them.

It was the guests finally who saved the day. They simply opened the door and pulled Lot back in. Then they focused on the crowd with the power of their presence. This was like a light blinding them and disorienting them. For a moment the townspeople were paralyzed, and then they drifted away.

The point had been made. This city was so wicked it needed to be destroyed. This family was to leave immediately, now, before the destruction. Yet, even here, Lot and his sons-in-law could not quite believe it. They had to be urged to go. In the morning the angels had to practically push them out of the house. And still Lot negotiated for going to a little city not quite so far away. He does not show himself here a strong or courageous leader, nor as a man of strong faith. Yet he and his family are finally urged to leave.

One wonders how Lot's wife felt at this time. Surely, you would think, she would be glad to go.

But it was she who turned and looked back.

This was in direct disobedience to the command not to look back. We wonder if this was such a terrible thing to do. We wonder if we have missed something. She, of all people, would be the one who would not want to look back.

There are salt-rock formations along the southern end of the Dead Sea and this story of Lot's wife may be an explanation of them. Further, it serves as an example of the consequences of disobedience to a command of God.

There are many lessons we can find in this story. God makes demands on all of us, the way he did on Lot and his family. This family was apparently the only good family in the city and they did not quite believe that destruction would really happen. They were all a bit recalcitrant.

When we do not follow God's plan, we may well be destroyed along with the wicked. Or, we may simply be stuck forever in our present position like Lot's wife. She would stay forever looking back.

Once we are urged by God to go forward we must never look back. The past is over, gone, never to come again. We have only the future to look to. Some of us, perhaps, dream of "what might have been," and sometimes, the "might have been" is totally unrealistic. If things had been different, they might well have been worse.

Dreams are not in themselves bad. Psychologists tell us that

dreaming and imagining the future can lead us to make plans that
make that future possible, within the parameters of God's plan.
But dreams of the past are futile since we cannot change a single
thing of the past. If we spend our time looking back, we may well
become like Lot's wife, left immobile on the way.

Discussion:

1. What do you imagine were the feelings of Lot's wife and her
   daughters that night in Sodom? How can you relate this to
   more modern incidents?
2. Do you think Lot's wife looked back out of curiosity? How
   do you picture this woman?
3. Is it more common for people to look to the past or to the
   future? What difference does it make in one's life?

SELECTED BY A SIGN

The Choosing of Rebecca

R EBECCA IS A CHOSEN WOMAN. WHEN WE MEET HER SHE IS doing a chore that daughters of families such as hers always did, going to the well to get water.

A stranger is there at the well, waiting. He had asked God for a sign to let him know which young woman God had chosen for his master, Isaac, another of God's chosen people. Rebecca speaks the exact words and does the exact actions that the servant had asked of God.

We also see that she is very beautiful and learn that she is from the right kind of family to be married to Isaac. This is clearly to be a marriage made in heaven.

We might wish that we could have asked Rebecca, "What do you think of this situation? Do you believe that this messenger is truly from God? Are you willing to follow this servant and marry his master, sight unseen?"

We cannot ask her, of course, but we do know that Rebecca chose to go. The servant had been concerned about that very question. What if the girl did not want to come? Apparently, she was not to be forced. Abraham must have realized that he was asking a great deal of anyone to leave family and home for sights unseen. As we see, Rebecca did have the final say. "Yes," she said. She would go and marry this Isaac.

The ancient Israelites did not have our modern ideas of a courtship and marriage based on mutual attraction. Marriages were usually arranged with or without consulting the young person. People thought of marriage not so much as a permanent love affair, but as a joining together of two families, of an attempt to combine the best possibilities and opportunities for all involved. It was hoped that love would come out of the mutual sharing that a marriage required. Frequently it did, but not always. Still, one could make the statement that there was probably as much love in marriages then as there is today.

Rebecca knew the marriage customs and the risks involved when she was given a choice. She chose to take the risk and that is one of the most significant things about her. She was a strong woman. Later we will see how she exercised her strength in her household.

Rebecca was chosen by God to be the mother in a family whose actions would have far-reaching consequences. She knew she was chosen and she took the risk and accepted it. She took a step into the dark knowing that God who chose her would be with her.

In many ways that is what happens to all of us. We are constantly being asked by God to do certain things. We do not get direct messages from him with angelic visitors. But neither did Rebecca for that matter. Her message came from a servant who was waiting at a well and it was delivered one day when she was simply doing her daily chores. That is exactly what happens to us. Someone we meet has a message from God for us. What is important is to recognize it for what it is. It takes sensitivity and alertness to see that God is asking something from us. Whatever he asks of us will require a risk-taking on our part, a willingness to take a chance. We will need to step out from our secure and safe little world where we are comfortable with doing what we are doing and move into another area where we are not secure and where we might well fail.

Rebecca's marriage could have turned out to be a disaster. She might have found Isaac a cruel and obnoxious person to live with. Her risk was high, accepting this unknown man. At least if she had stayed in her native village, she would have known the men there and, as beautiful as she apparently was, she might have been the choice of the best the village had to offer.

Even her family were less willing for her to go than she was to go. They asked the servant to allow her ten days in order to say her good-bye's, but Rebecca was willing to leave immediately.

There are many times when God calls us to do something that we temporize. Give me a little more time, we say, say ten more days. But we need to respond to God's call with alacrity. There is nothing more important in life that we can do than respond to God.

Discussion:

1. Do you admire Rebecca at this point in her life? How do you picture her in her home and family?
2. Can you give examples of times that God calls us to take a step into the dark?
3. What are some of the excuses we give for delaying our response to God? What might be our real reasons?

MOTHER OF TWINS

Rebecca and Her Sons

IN THE PATRIARCHAL LIFE OF THE ISRAELITES, THERE WERE dimensions defining the roles of men and women. They had no doubts about these roles; such things were part of the natural world, as they saw it. There was no Women's Liberation Movement in those days, but women have always found a way to equalize things. Rebecca was a woman who worked behind the scenes to manipulate both her husband and her children.

We are perhaps bothered by her obvious favoritism of her younger son, Jacob. But it is not hard to see why she preferred him. For one thing, the father Isaac seemed to prefer Esau, the man of the hunt, the more masculine of the two. We can imagine the father Isaac going off with Esau and spending all day hunting, only to return in the evening with the day's catch. Jacob, on the other hand, would have been at home all day with his mother, keeping her company and helping her around the house. As we see, Jacob even helped with the cooking, preparing the stew for which Esau sold his birthright.

That birthright was quite significant in the case of twins. In our day, with our very different customs, most families do not see the eldest son as the one who is entitled to the inheritance. Most American families are likely to divide the inheritance in some kind of equal fashion. Parents are anxious to avoid any kind of favoritism, even to their firstborn. In the event of twins, even though we know that one is born perhaps a few minutes before the other (and the twins themselves are not likely ever to forget which one came first, once they have been told), no one else seems much to care about that. They celebrate the same birthday and are treated as equal. How strong the tradition of first born among the ancient Israelites must have been to consider that the one who emerged first at birth be considered the inheritor and the other only a lesser member of the family. No wonder there was conflict between the two and no wonder that birthright was often on Jacob's mind.

The incident of selling the birthright for some stew did not seem to be taken seriously by Esau, yet Jacob never forgot it, nor did his mother. She wanted Jacob to have the blessing of his father before his father's death. This was a most sacred blessing and once given, even by mistake, could not be recalled. We are faced here with the very ancient, but still with us, concept of the sacredness and power of words. Once they have left a person's mouth, they take on a life of their own.

When it was time to do the deed and deceive Isaac, Jacob was hesitant. He did not seem to worry about what he was doing, only that he might be caught and call down upon himself a curse. A curse, like a blessing, would be powerful in itself; the curse could work its destruction. But Rebecca assured him that all would be well and if there was a curse, she would accept it. She probably knew by now that Isaac was not only blind but perhaps a little slow in thinking. It seems strange that he did not recognize the difference between the skins of animals and the feel of his own son Esau.

And so Jacob received the father's blessing, with the connivance of his mother. When he discovered the ruse, Isaac became very angry and Esau was naturally outraged. Esau knew that he had better not harm his brother while Isaac lived, but he could wait until after his death.

Rebecca watched this and knew exactly what was going to happen. Apparently Isaac did not. (We can well picture the situation: Isaac, the old blind man, is still nominally in charge, but it is Rebecca who runs things.) Rebecca went to Isaac and told him that she did not want their son Jacob to marry a woman of the Hittites. He should find a woman of her own people, and for that he should go and stay with his uncle Laban. Isaac agreed and sent Jacob on his way.

So our beautiful Rebecca has become a manipulative woman, dominating the lives of her husband Isaac and her sons Jacob and Esau. What she does can hardly be considered admirable. We feel sorry for the old Isaac duped by his wife. We are uneasy when we think of how Esau was tricked into giving up his birthright. We feel that Rebecca's favoritism went a little too far.

Yet what she was doing was acting, unwittingly, according to God's own plan. He never felt bound by any earthly ideas of birthrights and firstborns. Instead he chose whom he would. Frequently he chose exactly the ones we would not have chosen. He can make use of the foibles of human beings.

Maybe sometimes we need to remember this. God comes to us not only in his holy ones. He speaks to us not only through a Mother Teresa, but also through a bag lady or a gossipy neighbor. He knows what he is doing and can bring good and effect his plans through whomever he wishes.

Discussion:

1. List the outstanding qualities of Rebecca. Which of these do you see as admirable and which do you see as not admirable?

2. Is it common for a mother to favor one child over another? How do children react to any kind of favoritism?

3. What comments could you make about the relationship here of Rebecca and Isaac?

Genesis 29:15-30

THE OLDER PLAIN SISTER

Leah

J ACOB FOUND HIS WAY TO HIS UNCLE'S HOUSE. THE FIRST PER-
son he met of his uncle's household was Laban's daughter Rachel. It might well have been love at first sight. Rachel,
we learn quickly, was beautiful.

We also find out that Laban had an older daughter whose
name was Leah. She was not so beautiful and seems to have had
some problem with her eyes. (Some translations call her eyes weak,
while others call them pale.) But Jacob already loved Rachel and
would all her life.

We know how Laban took advantage of Jacob's work. He
would have to work seven years to win Rachel. He did so gladly;
he was so in love with her. It must have been a joy each day to see
her. And all this time, Leah was watching. She must have noticed
the light in Jacob's eyes each time he looked at Rachel. She must
have wished that he, or some other man, would look at her like that.

When the seven years were over, her father told Leah his
plan. As a dutiful daughter, she was required to go along with the
deception, of being given in marriage to Jacob instead of Rachel.

We wonder how she felt. She would, perhaps, have wanted

Jacob as her husband. But she was a true woman and what she wanted was not just to be married, but to be loved by her husband. She must have feared Jacob's anger when he realized that he had been deceived. (In a way, it serves Jacob right to be deceived, considering how he deceived his father with his mother's connivance.)

We also wonder how this could have happened. Apparently the bride would have been totally veiled until dark and Jacob did not know until morning that it was Leah he had slept with.

We can imagine the morning after the wedding. Jacob awakes to see Leah lying on the pillow next to him. He is amazed at first, then disappointed, and then totally angry. He gets up and runs to Laban, planning to have this out. Leah stays alone in the tent, in tears.

She knows that she has been used. She is legally and truly married to Jacob and he does not love her. This was not how she had hoped that her married life would be.

Later it is all settled. Jacob comes back to the tent at least somewhat mollified. He would be able to marry Rachel by the end of the week on condition that he work another seven years. Work does not bother him as long as he will have Rachel. He barely notices that Leah is still weeping.

That must have been a difficult week for her, having him spend it in anticipation of his coming marriage to Rachel. When he marries Rachel, Leah knows that already she is nobody in Jacob's life.

Yet she is the one who was able to bear children. She has son after son while Rachel, the loved one, remains barren.

To have a son was any woman's desire and delight and here Leah was far more blessed than Rachel.

Jacob still loves Rachel more, but he can not be unaware that it is Leah who was giving him sons.

Still, when eventually Rachel is blessed with a child who is named Joseph, that child quickly becomes the joy and darling of his father. Jacob learned well the lesson of favoritism from his mother Rebecca.

We cannot help sympathizing with Leah. She is the woman who is not loved, and the reason seems to have had little to do with herself. It is just that she is the older sister of a highly-favored younger sister.

There are several aspects of this story that we could dwell on. One would be the devastating effects of favoritism in families. It is certain that every person is naturally drawn more to one person than another, even in a family, but to act on that favoritism or to make others feel less worthy, can be disastrous. Frequently, as in this case, the favoritism had nothing to do with the personal qualities of the person. Yet it has an effect on those personal qualities. When persons feel unloved and rejected through no fault of their own, they quickly begin to think that they are somehow unlovable, not worthy of love and deserving of rejection. The weakened self-concept that results constricts them, keeping them from reaching out to others or from performing at their best.

We could also talk about how Leah was used by both her father and her husband. She knew that Jacob did not love her and she knew that he would never love her after he had been tricked into marrying her. The blame goes to her father who seems to be well skilled in taking advantage of people. Later, when she does the best that a good wife could do in those days, which is to produce sons, even that was not enough to win Jacob's love, although that was something she never gave up hoping for. Rachel, the loved wife, even envied Leah in her sons and told Jacob to give her one too or she would die.

In many ways this part of the story is hard for us to relate to. We no longer believe that a woman's only value is in her ability to have children, especially sons. Further we find it difficult to imagine a household where the man has two wives whom he must satisfy and where these two wives even give their maidservants to him so that they may also produce children. Yet we do know the effects of using other people for one's own advantage. This can cause anyone to feel less than a whole person.

Finally, we could discuss the sister relationship here. Sisters can be the world's best friends. Or they can be constantly competing with each other. One wonders whether Leah and Rachel would have been good friends if their father had not forced them into marrying the same man. Although Rachel is the beautiful daughter and much loved wife, we may feel closer to Leah. Perhaps that may be because we have all felt unloved and unlovable at sometime or other in our lives.

Discussion:

1. What do you imagine it was like living in the household with Leah and Rachel and all those children, not to speak of the servants?
2. Leah was in a situation that in the times she lived she could not escape from. What is to be said about the way modern women are able to escape from bad situations and yet choose to remain in them?
3. Is there still favoritism in families? If so, how can this be combated?

Genesis 31:25-35

THE BEAUTIFUL AND BELOVED

Rachel

T HE BIBLE, AS GREAT LITERATURE, IS FULL OF SERIOUS DELV-
ing into the human condition. It is also full of irony and
humor if we know where to look for it.

This story of Rachel is a masterpiece. We see her, the
younger sister, as the desired and favored. This is not at all unlike
the situation of Jacob; he too was the younger brother and favored.
As he deceived his father, he too is deceived by his father-in-law.

The image of Rachel that we are given immediately portrays
her as a woman who is so beautiful and so desirable that to work
to win her for seven years is nothing; in fact, Jacob loves her so
much that he finds seven years only a few days. He even agrees
immediately to work another seven years after he finds that he has
been deceived by Laban.

I suspect that any woman reading this passage feels a certain
amount of envy of Rachel; we would all like to be loved so much
that a man would do so much for us. And yet in other ways
Rachel's life was tragic. She waited years to have a child, while
watching her sister and even two maidservants have children by
Jacob before her. She was his beloved wife, but others gave him

33

children. She went to Jacob and complained so loudly that she
angered him. He shouted at her, "Who do you think I am, God?!"

It must have been a shock to this woman to find her Jacob
angry with her.

Later we see that when she is finally able to give birth to a
second son, Benjamin, it costs her her life. Rachel will die in childbirth.

We also see another image of Rachel. We know that her family still had not given up their pagan idols in favor of the God of
Jacob. When Jacob and his family choose to leave Laban — and
we say, it's about time! — Rachel does not want to leave without
the household idols. She does not even tell Jacob about it.

Her father is angry about Jacob's leaving. In fact Jacob had
hoped to slip off unnoticed. But Laban, searching as it were for a
reason to detain Jacob, notices that the idols were missing. He
hurries after Jacob and his entourage.

"Why did you steal the household idols?" he asks.

"We did not take them," Jacob retorts. He is so sure of himself that he even promises his father-in-law that whoever has sto-
len the idols will be punished with death — his beloved Rachel!

Laban searches everywhere for his idols. He cannot find them
in Jacob's tent nor in Leah's tent. He goes into Rachel's tent. She
is there sitting on a camel cushion. She remains sitting there, the
idols under her, and claims that she cannot rise; it was her time of
the month. She knows her father all too well. He will not insist that
she rise. He leaves without the idols. (Of course, for the Israelites
this story was very funny. These idols — supposedly gods! — were
hidden under a menstruating woman.)

So Jacob's big family finally was able to leave the home of his
two wives. One cannot help but feel a little sorry for Jacob. He
seems to have bitten off a little more than he could chew.

The story of Rachel brings us face to face with the strange

mystery of love. Rachel is loved and that love for her is strong enough to overcome many other obstacles. We see that she is beautiful when Jacob first meets her and he is smitten for life. He fell in love with Rachel and never fell out of love. His regard for her carried over into a special love of her sons. It was obvious that his love for Joseph and Benjamin was simply an extension of his love for Rachel.

How can we explain this? It could not have been beauty alone. We can imagine that as the years went by Rachel's beauty dimmed. The harsh climate and the hard work of women in those days certainly were not conducive to women's keeping their looks. But no doubt Jacob always saw her in his mind as the beautiful young maiden that he had first met when he fled his brother's wrath.

How strong and beautiful love is. And it seems to be given without being earned. This explains that strange phenomenon we often see — people caring for other people who seemingly have nothing to offer them in return. Mothers and fathers who never give up on their wayward children. Husbands and wives who spend years with incapacitated spouses. Friends who overlook a myriad of faults simply because they love one another.

Rachel is also the symbol of the chosen one. In some ways we are all chosen. There is something that we have been selected to do. And yet frequently, like Rachel, it seems that others can do it so much better, and that the day we are selected seems to be only the beginning of trouble.

Discussion:

1. How do you imagine life at the home of Leah and Rachel? What are your comments on their life style?
2. How do you think Leah felt about the kinds of things Rachel

did, like stealing her father's idols? How might she have responded?

3. Do you believe that Jacob's love was somewhat out of line,
   as he showed definite favoritism to one wife and her sons?

DISHONORED AND DEFILED

Dinah

JACOB WAS THE FATHER OF MANY CHILDREN, TOO MANY, WE might be inclined to think. He had sons by each of his two wives as well as by maidservants. According to the thinking of the times, a man who could claim a large number of persons of his own flesh and blood was considered wealthy and blessed by God. Our vivid imaginations, however, paint a picture of one problem after another with wives who envied each other, sons who seemed to be typical boys, always in trouble, and at least one daughter.

It is this daughter that we will concern ourselves with here. Daughters were often not mentioned, but she is mentioned because of the incident that would change her family's standing in the community.

Dinah was at least the seventh child of Leah, born after her six sons. In between the sons of Leah there were four sons born of maidservants. Dinah came into a household of apparently boisterous young men. After her there were two more sons, the two most loved sons, Joseph and Benjamin, born of Rachel. Our sympathies go out to Dinah in such a household.

It is no wonder that the story tells us she went to visit some of the women of the land. She must have longed to have a girlfriend or at least someone to share her thoughts with. It was while she was on her way that Shechem saw her, waylaid her, and raped her.

Dinah must have felt violated and defiled, but we do not really know how she felt. There is probably nothing more disturbing in this story than the fact that Dinah's feelings or wishes are never even considered. She is considered the property of her family. Her brothers are outraged because these strangers have taken what was not theirs.

Shechem, who raped her, must have felt remorse on having done so. We are told that he really loved Dinah and tried to win her affection. He went to his father and asked him to get this girl for him for a wife. It is ironic that he, the rapist, of all people, cared about Dinah's feelings. He wanted to marry her now, not because he needed to "make an honest woman" of her, but apparently because he loved her. No matter how high the bride price, he said, he will pay it.

Echoes of the past again. It was Dinah's own father, Jacob, who paid a very high bride price for his wives. He must have understood the feelings of this man. Jacob, in fact, seemed to be more calm and self-controlled than his sons were. It is the sons who demanded that Hamor and his son Shechem and his whole tribe be circumcised. While they were enduring the effects, Simeon and Levi took advantage of the situation and massacred the men and sacked the city.

Rape is a crime, but so is the crime of Simeon and Levi. Jacob, for his part, appeared to be more concerned with his standing in the community than any moral issues.

It is difficult to find anything to admire in this story. We can have a certain sympathy for only two persons: Dinah, who is never consulted about her feelings, and Shechem, the rapist. He was willing to make amends.

This story shows as others do in the Old Testament the low esteem in which women were held. They were valued the way one's property was, but they were not considered full human beings.

What happened to Dinah after this? We simply do not know. No doubt as a defiled woman she had to settle for a second-class husband. And surely she must have gotten married.

Making a good marriage was the goal of any young woman and families were much concerned about this. Not only would a good husband provide well for the woman, but coming from "good stock" would assure that children would be healthy and cared for too. The right marriage increased the fortune of the entire family. In this story we see that the sons do not consider Shechem acceptable as a husband because of his family and background, and not just because he raped Dinah.

A young woman was to hold herself ready for the right man to come along. From her childhood, her father had the duty to protect her so that she could be handed over untouched to her husband. We still have the ceremony of the father "giving away" the bride at the wedding ceremony. The young woman was property, but, even more, the fact of her virginity was to protect a man's other property. He wanted to be sure that the son who inherited his goods was truly his son.

This is one of the reasons why parents were not so concerned about their sons who strayed as they were about their daughters. But for many centuries, and sometimes even today, a young woman who was raped was considered damaged property and lived in shame.

Dinah herself was not allowed to make her own decisions. She was only a tragic and abused person, one of the millions of women through the centuries whose lives have been determined by their brothers and fathers.

Discussion:

1. How do you picture Dinah? Imagine her in the household of Jacob.
2. Based on your knowledge of human nature, do you think that Dinah would probably have married Shechem? Might this marriage have worked even though it started with a rape?
3. What do you think about the modern morality fostered by today's society? Does it raise or lower the position of women?

Genesis 38:1-30

A WOMAN WINS A GAME

Tamar

W HEN WE READ THIS STORY WE ARE PERHAPS SHOCKED. We hear how Judah's son Er was married to Tamar, but supposedly for some unspecified sin he died young. In the ancient world, unexpected death at any early age was considered the result of sin. According to the levirate law, if a man died without offspring, his brother was to marry the widow and produce offspring for life. The Jews in those days were not sure about an afterlife. The only way one could be immortal was through one's children. Thus, to die childless was to lose all opportunity for immortality.

Onan then was to marry his brother's widow. But apparently he did not want to produce children that would not be counted as his. He "wasted his seed on the ground" as the story tells us, and for that he was destroyed. It is important to notice that the sin here was failure to fulfill the levirate law, not Onan's sexual behavior. But Tamar still does not have children.

Judah had a third son named Shelah. He was still young and Judah was afraid that if he asked this son to marry Tamar, Shelah too would die. In those days, as today among some people, a

41

woman who had two husbands, both of whom died early, was to
be avoided. There must be something about her that caused death!

Judah did not refuse his son Shelah to Tamar; he just told her
to wait. She waited and waited. As the years passed, it began to
dawn on her that she was never going to have a husband to give
her children.

Then she decided that the only way to achieve what she
wanted was through trickery. Her trick worked; Tamar became
pregnant.

As soon as her pregnancy was evident she was accused of
immorality; her punishment was to be burning. One cannot help
but notice all the ironies of this situation. Her own father-in-law's
behavior, consorting with a woman whom he thought of as a prostitute, was not disapproved of, whereas Tamar's behavior was considered deserving of death. Yet Tamar had the upper hand; she
had Judah's seal, cord, and staff. He admitted the guilt of not giving her his son to marry, but the situation did not change. Tamar,
on her part, gave birth, not to one son, but to two.

Here is a woman who by hook or by crook wanted a child and
achieved what she wanted. Her whole worth as a woman was
wrapped up in her need to have children. She was certainly ill-used
by the men in her life. The story clearly tells us that her two husbands died because of their own sins, and yet she was somehow
tainted because of them.

What a strange mystery is the relationship of men and
women. How much they need each other, how much they comple-
ment each other, how much together they could do. And yet how
little they understand each other.

Since women alone can give birth to children, and the giving
of birth is such a significant event, many persons have wanted to
limit women to that function. When a society limits women that
way, a woman feels useless without the birth of a child. That was
certainly the case of Tamar.

We know that women are given as many gifts as men are. The differences in men and women are not in the gifts they are given, but in the way they are brought up to believe they can use their gifts. Some men, especially those of the ancient days, were so accustomed to seeing women as second-class creatures that they frequently underestimated them.

Yet Genesis shows us that women were not to be overlooked. Tamar is only one of a long line of women from the beginning of the world who managed to achieve what they wanted in one way or another. Very frequently they had to resort to trickery to get what they wanted; they could not compete in a more direct way. In their trickery they usually succeeded because men underestimated them.

When we look for a lesson in this story, we do not find behavior to be imitated. What we find is rather a commentary on life, even on modern life. A young woman may not wait along a street posing as a temple prostitute. But she may tell a man that he is the father of her child when she knows full well it is another man. Women will continue in such deceits as long as they do not have recourse to more direct routes to achieve their desires.

As long as women must rely on reluctant men, they will play games. One wonders if there ever will be a time when women can compete equally. Some, men and women, will say that women should not compete at all. Then women will have to go on playing tricks.

Discussion:

1. How do you feel about Tamar? Do you find her behavior totally unacceptable? Explain.
2. What do you think the people of those days who knew Judah

and Tamar thought of the situation? Was Judah laughed at and Tamar condemned?

3. Do women today still play tricks to get their way? If so, why? Do men ever play tricks?

THE CONNIVING WOMAN

Potiphar's Wife

A S WE READ THIS STORY, WE CANNOT BE EDIFIED BY POTI-
phar's wife. She was attracted to the handsome Joseph,
she wanted his attention, and she made her intentions
known to him. He spurned her. Because of his rejection, she accused him of attempting to rape her and as a consequence Joseph
was sent to prison.

This woman, whose name we do not even know, is the ar-
chetype of the dangerous woman who is the cause of the downfall
of a valiant man.

We cannot excuse her; yet, for all we know, Potiphar may
have been such a self-centered man that he paid little attention to
his wife. The story tells us that after Joseph took over his house,
Potiphar gave no thought to anything but the food he ate. Or,
Potiphar may have had other women.

How many incidents there are in the Bible of men and women
taking advantage of each other sexually. The sex drive is a strong
one and it is no surprise that throughout history many men and
women were not able to handle it well. However, it is one thing to
be weak and to fail and quite another one to be the cause of
another's disaster.

The penalty for adultery was death. Joseph knew that, but he was less concerned with the penalty than he was with the way his acquiescing to this woman's demands would be a betrayal to the master who trusted him. There seems to be little concern here simply with sexual morality.

We see Joseph as totally admirable. Even when he is sent to prison, he recognizes the hand of God. Potiphar's wife was certainly not acting according to God's commands, yet God was able to draw good from it. And Joseph had the spiritual insight to understand that.

Although we cannot excuse Potiphar's wife and what we know about her does not make her admirable, I am concerned that too many women are put into her class. Women through the centuries have been treated as though they were temptresses responsible for the downfall of men. It seems, however, that men have as often betrayed women as women have betrayed men.

The way our society is structured today, for all our modernity and liberation, it is still not so very different from the way it was at the time of Joseph in Egypt. It was then and is still to some extent today, considered appropriate only for the man to make the advance. Women were to wait until they were asked. No doubt many people through the centuries have found Mrs. Potiphar's behavior especially reprehensible because she was the one who made the advance. We easily mix morality with social custom.

Perhaps we must look to Joseph for the message. God, in his wisdom, allows many bad things to happen to good people for their own good. If Joseph had not gone to prison he would not have met the Pharaoh's cupbearer who eventually brought Joseph's ability to interpret dreams to the Pharaoh's attention. And because of that, as we recall, Joseph became the man in the kingdom next in power to the Pharaoh himself. Ultimately this position allowed him to become reconciled with his brothers and reunited with his father.

And what of Mrs. Potiphar? Did her husband really believe her story or had she tried this trick with other men? One wonders and we will certainly never know.

Later when Joseph became the Pharaoh's right hand man, Potiphar and his wife may have had dealings with him. As admirable a person as Joseph was we cannot imagine him revenging himself on her. We can only think that perhaps at one meeting or another they exchanged a look. Did Mrs. Potiphar look at him with fear, knowing that he was now able to destroy her if he wished? Did Joseph's look convey to her that all was forgiven?

If he did, we can be sure that that was the turning point in her life. If Joseph forgave her, she could probably then forgive herself.

Discussion:

1. What do you imagine the situation was like between Potiphar and his wife before they met Joseph? After they met Joseph?
2. How has the theme of the dangerous woman destroying the valiant man been used throughout history?
3. What can we learn from the way that this action of Mrs. Potiphar was actually the cause of greater things for Joseph?

PRIVATION AND PRIVILEGE

Pharaoh's Daughter

HE COMMAND WENT OUT THAT ALL THE BABY BOYS WERE TO be thrown into the water, while the girls could be permitted to live. This would not be the only time in Scripture when someone wanted to destroy baby boys; we are immediately reminded of the command centuries later of Herod in Jerusalem. Here, as in that story, we have someone intervening in the case of a special child.

Moses' mother would not, could not, allow her baby to die. He was a fine child, the story reads. She was to put him in the river; so she does. Only she puts him in a protective basket where he would be safe. Then she posts his sister along the river to watch and keep track of what happens to the baby.

Pharaoh's daughter, whose name we do not know, came along the river to bathe. She saw the baby, heard him crying, and decided to save him.

She knew very well he was a Hebrew baby.

Moses' older sister put in her appearance. "Do you want a nurse for him from among the Hebrew women?"

"Yes," Pharaoh's daughter answered. "Get one and I will pay

her." So, of course, the girl ran and got her mother. Moses' mother was thus able to not only save the life of her child, but also to be paid for it. She knew that eventually, when the child was weaned, she would need to turn him over to the house of Pharaoh.

The Scriptures say nothing else of this daughter of Pharaoh. Most of our images of her come from movies like Cecil B. DeMille's "The Ten Commandments" and not from the Scriptures. But we can imagine the situation quite well. Pharaoh's daughter probably knew that the woman nursing the child was the natural mother. Also she had no scruples about disobeying her own father's wishes, that all Hebrew boys be killed.

Her father must have doted on her and could deny her nothing. Or, he never paid much attention to what she did. In any case, she was a privileged daughter and could do as she pleased.

We are told that when the child grew up, his mother brought him back to Pharaoh's daughter and she brought him up in the court, even giving him his name.

The Pharaoh would have seen the boy around the court and since his daughter wanted him, did not object. It seems likely that Moses was a charming and intelligent youth. He would have been educated at the court, perhaps on an equal level with the Pharaoh's own sons.

It seems that Moses always knew his origin. He knew that he was a Hebrew and, although during his childhood, he was kept at the court and knew little of the sufferings of his people, he learned later on. And he had compassion on his people.

This story is interesting because it is a case of a man being saved by women. Moses' natural mother, his sister, and then his adoptive mother all protected him and kept him from being killed. We know that Pharaoh's daughter was compassionate, even if her father was not. We see that Moses, whatever else he learned at the court, learned compassion, probably from his mother.

So one day, when he saw an Egyptian striking a Hebrew, he defended his countryman and killed the Egyptian. But his deed was seen and he had to flee.

Later he met the seven daughters of the priest of Midian who were being bothered and hindered from watering their flocks by rough shepherds. He helped the girls and protected them from the shepherds.

They reported to their father that an Egyptian had saved them. Apparently Moses was still dressed like an Egyptian and no doubt spoke and acted like one.

That evening as they dined together he must have told the priest his story. Soon he settled down in the family and took one of the daughters, Zipporah, for a wife.

Moses is a good example of a person being brought up in two cultures, a situation that is often a cause of great conflict.

As we see often in the Scriptures, the woman that one marries is very significant in determining which culture one will live in and which God one will worship. Moses' wife was not a Hebrew, but she was clearly not an Egyptian either.

Moses knew his heritage and chose his own native culture. He would end up being one of the greatest leaders of his people.

But it is often, as it is here, the women who lead the way.

Women are usually the ones who preserve the culture and the faith of the families. It is mama who teaches the small child his prayers and the stories of his faith.

We can imagine Moses the baby imbibing the stories of his faith as he did his mother's milk. We can imagine that even as he lived in the court where the Egyptians worshiped many gods, somewhere deep in his consciousness he knew that none of them were the one true God, whose name was too sacred to speak, and whom he would eventually meet face to face on Mount Sinai.

Discussion:

1. Imagine the situation where Pharaoh's daughter meets the natural mother of Moses. How did they look at each other and what might they have said?
2. Do you know situations in which the women protect and save the boys and men? What are the aftereffects?
3. Is it more true today or less true that mothers are the carriers of the culture of a people?

FAMILY AFFAIRS

Miriam, Sister of Moses

MOSES WAS THE GREAT LEADER; HE HAD SPOKEN DIRECTLY with God. He had been chosen out of all the He-brews, indeed out of all human beings.

But he still had a family and, as usual, problems existed within his family. The whole world may praise a person, but to his own family, he is just a father, brother or son.

Both Moses' brother Aaron, the Levite who was selected to help Moses speak to the Pharaoh, and his sister Miriam, no doubt the same sister who watched him when he was pulled from the river by Pharaoh's daughter, were disappointed with him. He had married a Cushite woman.

They said, "Has Yahweh spoken to Moses only? Has he not spoken to us too?"

They were feeling somewhat less than pleased with all the adulation that Moses was receiving from the people. He wasn't even an exemplar of virtue, they said; he had married a non-He-brew woman.

So God, as it were, called a meeting of all three of them. He told them that it is true that he has spoken to all of them, but only to Moses has he spoken as he did. Other people have visions and dreams. Not so with Moses:

> "He is at home in my house;
> I speak to him face to face,
> plainly and not in riddles,
> and he sees the form of Yahweh."

God was angry and punished Miriam with leprosy. Aaron, for a reason not given, was not so punished.

Of all diseases, leprosy was the most feared. It could be compared to AIDS today. We now know that leprosy is not nearly so contagious as the ancients thought, but in those days, people were so afraid of contracting leprosy that lepers had to live apart from everyone else. Leprosy had the further effect of horribly disfiguring a person. To inflict leprosy on a person was, therefore, to give them a very terrible punishment. God was clearly trying to make a point.

However, Moses interceded with God. His brother and sister might complain about him, but his family ties were still very strong. He took advantage of his privileged position with God. Heal her, he begged.

God listened. He sent Miriam out from the camp for seven days and then brought her in. Apparently after that time, she was cured.

The people did not leave Hazeroth, where they were camping, until her return.

Is this simply a story of jealousy, of not being able to rejoice in the good fortune of another? It may be that. It is a very human story and there are others like it in the Scriptures: the case of the older brother of the prodigal son comes to mind.

Miriam was the good daughter. Aaron, like the older brother

of the prodigal son, was the good son. They had never broken the laws. Yet God chose Moses.

God has an interesting way of choosing people. Often he chooses the one we would not. Certainly he does not necessarily choose the "best" person. We have seen this again and again in the Scriptures.

In these days as women are slowly learning to find their role in life and in the world and in the Church, they must be careful not to choose simply whatever men have traditionally done. The issue is not to want to be what someone else is. The important thing is to do whatever one is called to do.

It is not that God does not choose women for important tasks in his work. He often does. But it is he who does the choosing.

Miriam's mistake was in thinking that somehow she was better, more deserving of being chosen than Moses was.

She would not likely have said what she did to another man; but Moses was just her brother. She could say what she wanted to him.

She did what many of us seem to want to do: she wanted to control God. What strange creatures we are. Somehow we think that we have to control the actions of God himself.

Discussion:

1. Do you feel sympathy for Miriam having a brother like Moses? Is it often difficult being in the family of a very famous person?
2. What do you think women are being called to do in the Church today?
3. What may be one reason why God often chooses the person we would not choose?

Joshua 2:1-21; 6:22-25

Rahab

W HEN JOSHUA'S SPIES WERE EXPLORING THE COUNTRY AT
Jericho, they looked for a place to stay, a place where
they would be safe and be able to find out the news,
learn about the country. What better place than the house of
Rahab, described in the story simply as a harlot. Since it was not
unusual for strange men to come to her house, it was the safest
place in town for them.

Although prostitution was extremely common in the ancient
Near East and was not considered immoral for most of the people,
it was forbidden to the Israelites. To the spies, therefore, Rahab
was something of an outcast, though not so to her own people. It
is impressive, therefore, that she should help these people.

Apparently she was given a special gift to recognize these
men as chosen people of Yahweh, the true God.

The coming of the spies did not go unnoticed. The king's
men had watched their arrival and suspected why they came. They
asked Rahab to send them out to them. Instead, she hid them under the straw on her roof. She claimed ignorance concerning the
men. She didn't know where they came from, she said, and then

she told them that they had already left. If the king's men hurried, they might still catch them.

Similar to saying, "They went that-a-way!"

As soon as the king's men left, she went up to the roof and made a bargain with the Israelites.

"I know that Yahweh has given you this land. When you come, spare all of my relatives and me. Swear that you will do it."

They did so, but demanded that she tie a red cord on her house, the same cord that she let down from a window on the outside of the wall to allow them to escape. Some scholars believe that this red cord symbolized her profession, similar to what we today call a red-light district.

The Israelites were not quite sure they believed her. They even told her that they would be freed from their oath if she told anyone else.

She told no one else. When the day came that the Israelites stormed the city of Jericho, they spared no one, except Rahab and all her family, as they had promised.

Rahab certainly acted courageously. It always takes courage to choose to act contrary to the way our countrymen act. Her risks were great. If her countrymen found out about the deal she had made, she would be killed by them. If the Israelites forgot their bargain or chose not to honor it, she would die with the rest.

This story has a happy ending, perhaps because her trust was more in Yahweh than in the people.

Here again we see how God chooses certain people to work his own plans. We know nothing further about Rahab: perhaps she married and settled down in Israel; perhaps she even went back to her old profession. We simply know that she had her brief moment on the stage of life and she played her role very well.

Rahab is the kind of person who lived at the edge of life. Her house was at the edge of the city, right next to the city wall. She was often apparently the first person that strangers to the city might visit. She offered a welcome kind of hospitality to ancient travelers.

As an unmarried woman running her own business, she was very independent. She had no difficulty responding to the king's men who came looking after strangers. And it is interesting that they never searched her house. They believed her when she told them that the men had left.

The Israelites did not approve of prostitution and in many passages of the Scripture, the turning away from God on the part of the Israelites was compared to turning to a prostitute. But God always looks deeper than human beings do, and he saw a good woman here, one that was worth saving. He tells us once again that he can use anyone he wishes to work his will.

Discussion:

1. If this story were being enacted today, who might the Israelites turn to?
2. How do you see the character and personality of Rahab?
3. Trust in other human beings is significant in this story. How do you know if you can trust another?

Judges 4:4-31

THE JUDGE AND THE HAMMER

Deborah and Jael

D EBORAH, WE ARE TOLD, WAS A JUDGE AND A PROPHETESS. She was the wife of Lappidoth but, as he is not mentioned elsewhere, we can conclude that his was not a significant position among the people. Deborah was a judge in her own right and a highly respected one at that.

She used to sit under a tree named for her, Deborah's Palm, and administer justice. But she didn't wait for people to come to her. She had no qualms about summoning the people to her and advising them, even in conditions of war, which sadly, even then, seemed to be rather constant situations among the Israelites.

They were, at this time, being oppressed by Jabin under the commander of his army named Sisera. This sad situation had gone on for twenty years.

Deborah sent for Barak and delivered a message from Yahweh to him: "Go with ten thousand men to Mount Tabor; there you will encounter him and defeat him."

Barak is willing to go only if Deborah comes with him. "If you will not," he tells her, "I will not go, for I do not know how to choose the day when the angel of Yahweh will grant me success."

Deborah tells him she will go, but that it will cost him. The glory will not be his; Yahweh will deliver Sisera into the hands of a woman.

No doubt Barak imagined that the woman receiving the glory would be Deborah herself, but, in fact, it would not be Deborah. On the field, Deborah gave Barak the command, even though Sisera was there with all his chariots, nine hundred of them plated with iron, and all his troops.

"This is your day," she told Barak.

And Barak and his ten thousand men charged down the mountain, sending Sisera and his men and chariots into a panic.

Barak and his men pursued them and slew them all. Except Sisera. He made his escape alone and on foot. Gone were all those precious chariots.

Sisera went to the tent of Jael, wife of Heber the Kinite, whose people were allies of Jabin's men.

Jael invited Sisera to come in and stay with her. He came in and she covered him with a rug, offered him milk to drink (the better to make him drowsy), and then stood at the door of the tent as he had asked.

"Tell them," he told her, "if they ask, that there is no one here."

She nodded. Sisera felt relieved. After the horrible loss of his men and chariots, the long run of escape, he now felt safe. He hid under the rug and fell asleep.

This was what Jael was waiting for. She took up a mallet and a tent peg and drove it through his temple into the ground, killing him. Then she waited until Barak arrived.

We do not know Jael's motivation. We know that she could be accused, in Ancient Middle East customs, of violating the rules of hospitality. But apparently she knew what she needed to do.

The story is not yet over. After this great victory, the Israelites rejoiced and sang a song especially composed for the occasion. Scripture scholars recognize this as one of the most ancient songs of the Bible. It praises God for the victory and then retells the story, adding a few invented details:

> "Through her window she leans and looks,
>   Sisera's mother, through the lattice:
>   'Why is his chariot long in coming?
>   Why are the harnessed horses slow?'
> "Among her princesses the wisest one answers,
>   and she to herself repeats,
>   'They are gathering, doubtless, sharing the spoil:
>   a girl, two girls for each man of war;
>   a garment, two dyed garments for Sisera:
>   a scarf, two embroidered scarves for me!'"

But, of course, Sisera will never come home and there will be neither spoils nor rejoicing among his people.

What a story of women! Sisera was, as Deborah foretold, delivered into the hands of a woman. And in the end, his mother and the other women are all sad and disappointed.

The Israelite army comes across very weak here compared with the strength of these two women. Barak will not even go to battle without Deborah. And there is an irony in the fact that a woman, a foreigner, should be the one to finally kill Sisera.

Still Barak's attitude toward Deborah gives a vivid picture of the great respect in which she was held among the people. Further, Jael was honored and praised in the song as one of their saviors. Both women show themselves as sensible women who knew what they needed to do and did it. They are both self-assured and willing to do whatever is necessary.

Discussion:

1. Compare Deborah and Jael. In what ways are they alike or different?
2. How do you think Lappidoth felt when Deborah informed him that she was going to go off with Barak and his men because they could not fight without her?
3. Read the song of Deborah and Barak. What impresses you about this song?

THE POWER OF WOMEN

Delilah

S AMSON WAS A WILD MAN. HE WAS DIFFERENT; HE DID EVERY-
thing to excess; no man could outfight him. Yet he was
manipulated by more than one woman.

Before his birth, Samson's mother was barren, in those days
the greatest misfortune that could befall a woman. She longed for
a son.

An angel appeared to her, and later to her husband, and told
them to prepare themselves for a special birth. They were to watch
what they ate and drank and after his birth never cut their son's
hair. This was to be a sign of his total dedication to God.

Samson was born. It is likely that his parents were much older
than the typical age when their son was born. He grew rapidly and
he grew strong and soon they had little control over him. He went
to a village of the hated Philistines who had been oppressing the
country for forty years and there he noticed one of the daughters.
He liked her and he wanted her for his wife.

Although his relatives objected, Samson insisted. He apparently was accustomed to getting his way.

Along the way he fought and killed a lion with his bare hands.
This was only the beginning of his many feats of strength.

Samson liked riddles and he gave a riddle to his wife's countrymen. They could not figure it out, so they went to his wife.

She wheedled it out of him: "You only hate me, you do not love me."

She wept on his neck for seven days and he finally told her and she immediately told her countrymen.

Samson was so angry that he killed thirty men to pay his side of the riddle, and went back to his father's house. His wife was given to the best man of his wedding.

This wife's name is not even given, but it is easy to imagine her. She was selected by Samson and we are told twice that he liked her. We are not told how she felt, but women in those days often had little choice in their husbands. It is not surprising, however, that she should feel more loyalty to her own countrymen than she did to Samson.

Still Samson was willing to give her a second chance. He came to see her, carrying a kid as an offering. Her father would not let him in; she was now the wife of one of his companions. However, Samson could have the younger daughter if he wished.

That was just too much. Samson responded by destroying the crops of the Philistines and then burning his wife and her whole family.

Samson was not a man to be trifled with.

Later Samson, who clearly liked women, fell in love with another Philistine woman, the famous Delilah. Her people asked her to find out the source of his great strength. The way the story reads, it seems that Samson himself is not quite sure of the source of his strength, namely that it is in his uncut hair; but that is only symbolic of his relationship with God. It is God ultimately who is the source of his strength and it will last only as long as God chooses.

In the end, Delilah too betrays him and Samson is taken captive by the Philistines who treat him very badly.

However, he has his day. In the end, Samson, whose hair has grown back, turns back to God, and in the final act of his life, pulls down the building and destroys himself and many of his enemies in the process.

Samson dies as he has lived.

Samson is one of those larger than life characters that are often found in the Bible. He is a reckless man and a womanizer. Yet God, we are told, used him to help the Israelites achieve some independence from the Philistines, their perpetual enemies.

Samson is known for his strength and there are no Philistines who can outfight him; they cannot even outwit him without the help of their women. It is through women that he is brought down.

This story could be classified as another case of a valiant man deceived and destroyed by a conniving woman. That is one reading of it. There are other ways to view the story, however: women's only way to fight must be with their feminine wiles since they cannot outfight men physically. Women are far more often deceived and destroyed by men than men are by women.

But let us allow the story to stand as it is. It is hard for us to admire either Delilah or Samson's wife. What we can consider though is how women have and use power.

Men's power is often more straightforward, physical, and brutal. Women's power is exercised through gentle loving ministrations, teasing and begging, verbal assaults. This is true even today. Few men can hold out against the women whom they love and who love them.

This power can be used to destroy others, but it need not be. Women can also use that power to build and strengthen their men, give them courage and emotional support, gently correct their ways, even humanize them.

The saying, "Never underestimate the power of a woman," holds true today, as it ever did. Ultimately, when a woman really

wants something, she is very likely to achieve it, even over very
powerful men.

Discussion:

1. Imagine Samson's mother: how do you think she felt as she
   observed her wild and untamable son, knowing as she did
   that he was somehow a person chosen by God, even an-
   nounced by angels?
2. Imagine Samson's wife: why did she choose to betray him
   and how might she have felt when he returned to see her, carrying a gift?
3. Imagine Delilah: how would she have felt afterwards, when
   Samson's eyes were plucked out and he was mistreated? How
   would she have felt at his death?

IN-LAWS WHO LOVE EACH OTHER

Ruth and Naomi

RUTH WAS A MOABITE, A FOREIGNER AND A WORSHIPER OF false gods. She had married the son of Naomi and Elimelech, Israelites from Judah who had gone to Moab to escape a famine.

But life in Moab was not good for them either. Elimelech died and so did their two sons. Naomi was left alone with her two daughters-in-law, Ruth and Orpah. Naomi decided to go back to her home, because she had heard that God had heard his people's prayer and there was food there now.

We are told all of that in the first paragraph of this book of the Bible, but what a lot of woe is packed into it: the famine, the leaving of their home country, the loss of their men.

Naomi looked at Orpah and Ruth. "Why don't you go back to your people?" she asked. "I cannot give you new husbands."

Orpah listened and grieved, and then went back to her own people.

Not so Ruth. Ruth told her clearly that she would stay with Naomi no matter what:

"Wherever you go, I will go,
wherever you live, I will live.
Your people shall be my people,
and your God, my God."

And so they went. And what a sad return it was. "Don't even call me Naomi anymore," Naomi said. "Call me Mara (bitter)."

This bitterness was not to last. Ruth was not content merely to weep and lament her bad fortune. She decided to glean in the fields, seizing an opportunity to find not only food, but also perhaps a new husband there.

Gleaning was common among the Israelites and it was expressly allowed by the Law. Farmers were told not to reap fields to the extreme, but were to allow some plants to remain behind for the poor, resident aliens, orphans, and widows. Ruth fit this category quite well.

Boaz, the farmer whose field she approached, noticed her and was immediately attracted to her. He told her not to glean elsewhere; he would look after her.

Boaz was a kinsman and, as Naomi pointed out, he had right of redemption over her, although there was a closer relative with such a right. This meant simply that Ruth belonged to that relative along with the land and property that had belonged to Naomi's husband.

Time went by; Ruth worked every day in the fields until the end of the harvest. As usual, Boaz and his household held a party at the threshing time, a time of celebration for the harvest. With Naomi's encouragement, Ruth went to the party, dressed in her best. She waited, however, until Boaz had eaten and drunk well and was in a very happy mood.

He slept and she slept next to him, offering as it were a proposal of marriage.

Boaz was pleased because he had been attracted to her, but

it does not seem that he would have acted on his attraction if Ruth had not made the first move.

It all turned out well. Boaz won the right of redemption, and before witnesses "bought" Ruth and married her. The wedding was celebrated with great joy and soon Ruth gave birth to a son who was called Obed, destined to be the grandfather of David, and an ancestor of Jesus.

What a beautiful story of love this is. We find no bickering here between mother-in-law and either of her daughters-in-law. Apparently they both loved her, but Ruth especially loved her enough to want to stay with her. As they moved back to Judah they acted more like mother and daughter than like in-laws. Ruth even chose the God of Naomi, and this in spite of the fact that Naomi felt that Yahweh had turned his hand against her.

As women, they knew that they needed the help of men and clearly Ruth was hoping to marry again. She would have a new mother-in-law if she did, but that was not a problem for Naomi. Naomi rejoiced with her and was willing to give her up. We often overlook how difficult this may have been for Naomi. Ruth had been such a good support for her.

It is also significant that Ruth was a Moabite, thus making Jesus' ancestor a pagan. She converted and became a devout Jew, but perhaps she still retained many of her foreign customs. No one can change them completely.

We know something else about this situation. It is something of a Cinderella story. Ruth was poor (as most widows were poor in those days, having lost their means of support). She was noticed by the wealthy man who went out of his way to offer her kindness beyond the call of simple care for the poor. He even had her eat with him and his men and offered her protection.

But after that he made no other move. This was not the handsome prince who went throughout the kingdom to find her. One gets the impression that were it not for Ruth's and Naomi's actions, once the harvest was over, they would have lost track of one another.

Ruth and Naomi were not about to let this prime specimen of a husband escape. They used a little rather daring initiative, daring enough that Boaz insisted that she slip out before morning.

Women, even dependent as they were in those days, could not just allow things to happen. They needed to take the initiative if necessary, and in this story as in many others of the Scriptures, they did. Ruth is an example of a loving, faithful, and quite strong woman.

Discussion:

1. Why do you think God chose a foreign woman to be the ancestor of Jesus?
2. Do you think this picture of a mother-in-law and daughter-in-law relationship is very unusual? Where do you think all the mother-in-law jokes come from?
3. What do you make of the initiative Ruth displayed in order to get Boaz to marry her?

SINGING FOR A SON

Hannah

ERE WE HAVE WHAT WE FIND ELSEWHERE IN THE SCRIP-tures the barren woman who wants only to have a child. Yet Hannah is more fortunate than most. Her husband, Elkanah, loved her as she was. He had another wife, Peninnah, who had many children, but Elkanah did not prefer her. Peninnah would taunt Hannah, but Elkanah never did.

No doubt Hannah's barrenness was a source of pain at all times, but it was especially poignant when the family went up to the temple to offer sacrifice. Then Elkanah would give several portions to his other wife for herself and her children. But to Hannah he gave only one. She would weep and not eat, believing as she did that her barrenness was an affliction from Yahweh.

Elkanah would try to console her. "Am I not more to you than ten sons?"

But Hannah was not to be consoled. She wanted a son with all her soul, she wanted a son with all her heart, she wanted a son so badly that if Yahweh gave her one, she would give him to the Lord.

She made her prayer before Yahweh; Eli, the high priest,

noticed her praying although he could not hear the words. With her under-the-breath murmuring, he thought she was drunk and reproached her.

She defended herself: "I am not drunk. Do not take me for a worthless woman. I am only speaking from the depths of my grief."

Eli then told her, "Go in peace, and may God grant you what you so desire."

When she went away she felt different. Her depression lifted and she felt an inner peace, a daring to hope that God would indeed grant her what she desired.

They returned home the next day and very quickly afterwards she found herself pregnant. When their son was born, she named him Samuel, since he was one asked from God.

One can imagine Hannah cooing over her son, knowing that he was given to her for only a little while. She had promised him to the Lord and she would keep her promise. But after waiting so long for him, it was going to be difficult to give him up.

A year later when her husband and the family went up to Shiloh for their annual sacrifice, Hannah did not go with them. She said that she needed to wait until he was weaned.

We also can well imagine that she was not yet ready to give him up. Perhaps she felt that if she went up to the temple with her babe in arms, she would have to leave him there. Better not to go just yet.

But little Samuel grew and became strong and it was time to wean him. This may have been as long as two years later. Now Hannah knew she could put off her sacrifice no longer.

She took him to the temple with the required sacrificial offering and brought him to Eli. She left Samuel in his care.

Did Samuel cry when she left? Did Hannah cry? We do not know. We only know that, even if she cried, she also sang a song of praise to Yahweh.

Her song is one of exultation in the Lord, with complete emphasis on him as the mighty One who chooses and disposes as he sees fit, and holy is his name. The song reminds us of the song of Simeon in the temple when Jesus was presented, and of Mary herself in her Magnificat.

What an act of faith and sacrifice it was for Hannah to give this son to God. Yet her song speaks only of the greatness of God. Though her heart may break, her trust is ever strong.

Hannah was a normal human mother and to give her only son, whom she received after so many tears and so many years, was certainly difficult. But Hannah also knew, through her deep faith, that God was calling this son Samuel to a special service. In the Scriptures it frequently happens that persons are chosen by God even before they are born. They are destined for a special purpose; they have a special calling. This is certainly the case of Samuel.

Every mother has eventually to give up her children. Most mothers do not have to give them up so young, but eventually they must all be given up. It is a mistake to hang on to them. It is a mistake to see their leaving home to answer whatever their own call is as a betrayal. Children are never given to keep; they are only lent to parents for a while.

This is very hard for many parents. Some feel a loss of love when their children marry and choose other persons to be their chosen loves. But the sons or daughters who give their love to another are not rejecting their parents. Their hearts are expanding, able to take in new persons.

Parents would do well to follow that example, to take in new sons and daughters in the persons of the new in-laws.

It is also difficult when sons and daughters choose a style of life that their parents would not have chosen for them. Parents know that their children must respond to their own calling, whatever it may be. But how they would prefer that calling to be one that they can relate to.

It is nearly impossible for parents to be objective about their children. What their children become and do is always a part of them. The positive side of this can be lifelong care and support, no matter how far away the children go. The negative side can be a constant feeling of rejection, guilt, and reproach, over what the children are doing.

These reasons point out in clearer light how very heroic was the song Hannah sang after her very heroic action. We are told in 1 Samuel 2:11. "Then she left for Ramah, but the boy stayed to minister to Yahweh in the presence of Eli the priest."

We wonder if she looked back as she went. No doubt she did and waved, and Samuel raised his chubby little hands in a bye-bye.

She walked home with an aching heart, but with a deep faith and trust in God.

Discussion:

1. Describe your image of the family of Elkanah with his two wives, one with children, and one without.
2. Have you ever prayed for something and experienced deep in yourself that the petition would be granted? How did that make you feel?
3. Do you sympathize with Hannah in her attempt to hold off a little while the giving up of her son?

1 Samuel 18:17-27; 19:11-17

WIFE OF DAVID

Michal

I T COULD NOT HAVE BEEN EASY TO BE DAVID'S WIFE, NOR THE
daughter of Saul. Saul was the king of Israel and by this
time quite jealous of the up and coming David. David, on his
part, was wary.

Michal's older sister, Merab, had been promised to David,
but David stated that he was unworthy of marrying the daughter
of the king. Perhaps he really wanted to marry her and perhaps he
didn't. No one knows what Merab thought. In the end, it didn't
happen. When the time came she was given to Adriel in marriage.

One can imagine Michal observing all this. She was the
younger sister, probably quite young, and she was watching with
big eyes this handsome and brave young man who was promised
to her older sister. The Scripture tells us plainly, "She fell in love
with David."

She must have been quite happy when her sister was given
to another man. Now the road was open to her.

She could not hide her love. The word was brought to David
himself and he was quite pleased. It is easy to envision through
David's eyes, this young girl, just beginning to blossom. She must

77

have been quite beautiful and as a daughter of the king, David was flattered by her attention.

Yet David knew that Saul would demand a price if he was to be allowed to marry Michal. Through servants the price was named: the death of a hundred Philistines (the Scriptures say a hundred foreskins of the Philistines — trophies, reminding us of the custom of bringing in scalps).

We are also told in 18:25 that Saul was hoping and expecting that David would fall by the hands of the Philistines, so jealous of him was he by now.

On his part, David was delighted by the demand. Fighting was one of the things he knew and apparently loved best. He also really wanted to be the king's son-in-law. So he and his men set off and killed not one hundred, but two hundred Philistines.

It was enough. Michal was married to David, the man that she loved.

She had a chance to show her love later when Saul made an attempt on David's life. Michal warned David to leave. This is more significant than might appear on the surface. Not only did she choose her husband over her father, but her father was the king of the land.

When her father asked her why the trickery (she had fixed the bed to make it look like David was there), she claimed that David forced her to do it. In reality, it was entirely her own decision.

But David seems to have forgotten Michal later. He spent so much of his time away from home that eventually Saul gave her to another man to marry. David then, apparently without a backward glance, married Abigail and Ahinoam. Later, as we know, David had many other women, including the famous Bathsheba.

Michal then was for a time just the daughter of a king who served a useful purpose, as daughters of kings have done for centuries.

This would be neither here nor there if it weren't for the fact that we know that she genuinely loved David, and this in spite of the fact that David hardly deserved her kind of love.

Why do women so often fall in love with men who are only going to hurt them? Is it true that love is unpredictable, that we have no control over it, and that it is often a source of pain to us?

What happens when we fall in love?

It seems that the attraction to another person which happens when we fall in love is based on something deep within ourselves. A need is fulfilled in some way.

Michal, the younger sister, may have been longing for the great adventure in her life. Maybe she was wise enough to know that marrying David would only bring her pain, but she wanted it anyway.

Maybe she gave more to him than she ever realized, more than he also realized.

Maybe in later years as David looked back over his life and saw how often he had betrayed and been betrayed, he reflected that Michal's love was the best and purest he had had.

Discussion:

1. What do you think of David? Why is this story of David so different than we often think of him?
2. How do you picture Michal when she was married to David? How do you picture her in the later years when she was married to another man?
3. Why do women often marry men whom they know will hurt them and may even leave them?

BATHING BEAUTY

Bathsheba

T HIS IS ONE OF THE BEST KNOWN STORIES IN THE BIBLE. IT WAS
a cool evening and Bathsheba was bathing. No doubt
she was following her usual routine. But this evening she
was being observed by, of all people, David, the king of Israel, who
was strolling on the roof of the palace after having rested.

We are told only that she was very beautiful.

David could not stop looking at her. He decided that he must
know more about her.

He made inquiries and learned that she was called Bathsheba,
she was Eliam's daughter, and she was married to Uriah, the
Hittite.

David decided that he must have her. He had her brought to
him and soon they slept together. The story is told in three verses
in the Scriptures.

But what a story, and yet how ordinary. Unfortunately, kings
and emperors and presidents too have often felt that among their
other powers was the right to have any woman they wanted, married or not.

We know little of how Bathsheba felt. We do not know if she

was flattered when the messengers arrived at her door and told her the king wanted to see her. Did she have any doubts about what the king wanted?

Bathsheba's husband, Uriah, was away fighting at this time.

We do not know how long or how often she stayed with the king while Uriah was away. We only know that sometime later she sent him a message: she was pregnant.

The next part of the story gives us the impression that David was not at all anxious to assume paternity for the child. He called for her husband Uriah and asked about the war. He told him to go home then and enjoy himself. Apparently he expected Uriah to go home and sleep with Bathsheba; that way, the child would be thought of as his.

Or was it to protect Bathsheba's reputation?

In any case, Uriah did not go home; he slept by the palace door.

This news was brought to David who asked him why. Uriah told him that he could not go home and enjoy himself while both the ark and the men were lodged in tents.

David could not argue with that. He told him to stay at the palace and that evening they ate and drank together. David gave him enough wine that Uriah got drunk, but he did not go home.

David now knew he had to take more drastic measures. He sent a letter to Joab, the commander, and told him to place Uriah in the thick of battle where he was likely to be killed.

And so he was. Joab understood that David wanted Uriah killed and he coached his messenger that if David was angered by the news of the battle, the messenger should just tell him Uriah was killed. The news would mollify him.

That was exactly what happened. David was now happy that Uriah was out of the way.

Bathsheba too heard of the death of her husband. We are told that she mourned for him and when the period of mourning was over, David called for her and she became his wife and had a son.

We still do not know how she felt about it all. Was she merely the victim of the men in her life? Or did she hate David for what he had done to her husband and to her?

Apparently she had been the one and only wife of Uriah, whereas with David, she was one among the many women of David. David may have loved her, at least for a while.

But he was the cause of the death of her son.

Again the emphasis is on David, how he begged for the life of his son, but the son died anyway. This was in direct punishment for his sin.

Bathsheba too must have mourned her son. She had to pay a heavy price for being David's wife.

We are told that later David consoled Bathsheba and she had another son, this one, Solomon, who was to become a very famous king.

How did Bathsheba feel as the years flowed by and she watched her son grow to maturity?

God works in strange ways many times, even perhaps most of the time. What began in sorrow and pain and sin would end in rejoicing. David with all his faults and sins was a man much loved by God. He it was who was a chosen person.

Once more we are faced with God's way of choosing people. Sometimes he selects the weak and ignorant. Sometimes he selects natural leaders. Sometimes he selects those who can barely keep their feet on the high road, who will need to be sent prophets to straighten them out.

God also chooses people through other people, and he does this when the people themselves do not know that they are thus being chosen.

Perhaps David thought little of God or God's will as his lust insisted on having Bathsheba. Yet she was chosen to be the one who would be the mother of Solomon.

Discussion:

1. How do you picture Bathsheba before David came into her life? How do you see her after he came into her life?
2. Do you see Bathsheba as a weak or a strong person? Explain.
3. Why do you think David is named by Jesus himself as a man after God's own heart?

BROTHERLY LOVE

Tamar, the Violated

THIS IS THE SECOND WOMAN WE HAVE MET IN THE SCRIPTURES whose name was Tamar. Neither of them had an easy life.

This Tamar was the full sister of Absalom and the daughter of Maccah. She was the half-sister of Amnon.

We are told simply that Tamar was very beautiful. Like his father, David, Amnon had to have a beautiful woman when he saw her, no matter what the consequences or the circumstances.

Amnon was in love with Tamar and seeing her every day was more than he could bear. The Scriptures say that he was "so obsessed with his sister Tamar that it made him ill."

His friend Jonadab was very shrewd and quickly learned what was going on. He had a suggestion for Amnon: Pretend to be sick and take to your bed. When your father comes to see you and wants to know what is wrong, insist that Tamar tend you and bring you food. Only from her hands can you eat.

Tamar did as her father asked and prepared the food in front of Amnon.

We can imagine this scene with Amnon watching her every move from the bed.

But that was not enough. When she brought him the food, he would not eat. He insisted that everyone leave and that Tamar feed him personally. When she drew near him, he grabbed her arm and told her what he really had in mind.

She was horrified. To sleep with her brother, even half-brother, was too much. But Amnon would not listen to her; he overpowered her and raped her.

As soon as he did, he now felt a loathing for her. He hated her as much as he had once loved her.

Amnon drove her from the room and bolted the door behind her. She wept and wailed and soon everyone knew what had happened. David was very angry, but he did not want to punish Amnon his firstborn. Absalom was so angry that he would not speak to his brother.

Two years later, Absalom arranged for Amnon to be killed. Because of this Absalom had to leave for three years and the king mourned; he had, in fact, lost both of these sons.

And what happened to Tamar? She was probably pitied by some and blamed by others. This is the story of most women who are raped. There are always some who believe that it must have been at least partially their own fault. And there are others who pity them, but still see them as damaged goods, not worthy now of making a good marriage.

It is also significant that after the rape, Amnon hated Tamar. Why was this? Did he see her as the cause of his evil deeds?

How often in the past women were considered the snare of the devil for valiant men. This is similar to what happens when persons cannot control their drinking: they are likely to call alcohol "demon rum." How easy it is to blame the object or the victim of one's obsessions.

Here Tamar is both victim and object. Why was Absalom so angry with his brother? Likely it was because he had taken advantage of his sister, and women were objects to be protected by their brothers and fathers.

What of fathers? David had his hands full with the actions and problems of his children: his daughter violated, his sons at war with each other.

It is hard not to think that this is not surprising for a man like David who himself took a long time to learn how to control himself.

This entire story of Tamar and her half-brothers is one that is hauntingly familiar to people today. These very same problems come up again and again. Many fathers and brothers no longer believe that they must fight to protect their sisters and daughters, although something of this still exists in several countries. Even in the United States, the tendency to protect is strong.

Many a young man learns that it is not wise to date the sister of his best buddy. Or if he does, he must treat her with the greatest respect and consideration if he values his friendship with his buddy.

Is the slow loss of this protection in our society good or not? It is hard to say. Many women feel pleased to be cherished and cared for by their men, but often the price of being cared for is too high. It may well mean the loss of their own independence and opportunity to develop their own gifts.

We have not yet come to terms with this.

Discussion:

1. As you read this story of Tamar and Amnon and Absalom, what are your feelings? Outrage, sorrow, or some other emotion?

2. Can you imagine this household with all of this going on? All of these main characters were quite young. Could David be considered a biblical parent of teenagers? As such, do you have some sympathy for him?
3. What you think Tamar did with the rest of her life? How did she feel with her brothers warring with each other?

THE QUESTIONING QUEEN

Sheba

SOLOMON WAS KING. HE WAS KNOWN FAR AND WIDE AS A WISE man as well as a great builder, shipowner, and wealthy man. We are told that he equipped his fleet and his seamen went to Ophir and brought back four hundred and twenty talents of gold. This money would have been in exchange for goods that he sold. While they were selling, the merchants were no doubt telling of the greatness of their king.

Solomon's fame spread throughout the world of his time and soon the Queen of Sheba heard of him. Sheba was the name given to the region that is now probably Yemen, according to Scripture scholars.

The Queen was much interested. If Israel had such a great and wise king, and so many goods to sell, she reasoned, they no doubt had money to buy others. This could be a profitable deal.

But before trading she wanted to find out first hand just how wise and how great this king was. The way to do this would be to mount a mission.

The Queen herself came. This is most unusual. Rarely do we hear of kings visiting each other and almost never do we hear of queens.

This queen was apparently a woman of both power and wisdom herself. She came, the Scriptures say, to test him with difficult questions. But she also brought immense riches, camels laden with spices, gold and precious stones.

The king and queen gave gifts to each other. Then they took time to talk and the Queen of Sheba was much impressed by the king's prosperity and the organization of his kingdom.

All the stories she had heard about him were true, but they were only the half, she said. The king was even greater than she had been led to believe.

We are told that she opened her mind freely to him and Solomon had answers for all her questions; none was too obscure for him.

How sad that we are not given even a sample of the kind of questions she asked Solomon. Nor are we given any idea of how she impressed the king. However, the fact that she is mentioned is told as a proof of the greatness of Solomon that one such as the Queen of Sheba should come and see him personally.

This queen makes her appearance on one page of the Scriptures and then she is gone. We hear nothing more of her. But she is the model of all wise and determined women. When such women know what they want, there is little that can stop them.

The Queen of Sheba was a seeker after the truth and she sought it wherever she could.

As one looks through the years of history, one is often struck by the fact that, although women are rarely mentioned as leaders or rulers, they are often there side by side with the men, seeking the truth and cutting through the darkness to find the light.

The Queen of Sheba was apparently one of those fortunate women who were given an opportunity to develop their gifts.

We cannot help but wish that most women had more opportunities to use their talents. God seems to be very evenhanded in the way that he distributes his gifts: to men and women alike, to rich and poor, to persons of all classes and nationalities. It is not God who prevents their use, but human beings who do.

Unfortunately so often talent is never used because persons are not given the opportunity, or someone has led them to believe that their role in life is to do something else.

Often these persons are women. One wonders how many peasant women in history had brilliant minds but never learned even to read. How many women who were gifted were encouraged not to think of going to medical school; it would be too hard for them. How many women who could have been leaders and rulers were only allowed to be secretaries and assistants. How many God-given talents were lost, wasted, or totally frustrated.

We do not know if the Queen of Sheba was a good queen. Through history, queens have a mixed rating, like kings: some were very good, some were very bad, and others were simply mediocre.

It seems that there are not yet enough models for women as to how to play, in a feminine way, roles that were considered masculine.

Discussion:

1. How do you picture the Queen of Sheba? What would her life be like?
2. Picture the meeting between Solomon and the Queen. What kinds of questions might they have asked?
3. Imagine this queen returning to her own country. Might her life have been changed because of having met and talked with Solomon?

I Kings 16:29-32; 19; 21

TROUBLE IN ISRAEL

Jezebel

A HAB, WE ARE TOLD, "WAS WORSE THAN ALL HIS PREDECES-
sors. The least he did was to follow the sinful example
of Jeroboam son of Nebat: he married Jezebel, the daughter of Ethbaal king of the Sidonians, and then proceeded to serve
Baal and worship him."

With that we are introduced to the infamous Jezebel.

She has become known as an evil woman, one that caused a
great deal of trouble for the true faith in Israel. Not only did she
set up Baal to be worshiped, but she tried to exterminate all the
prophets of Israel. Obadiah, master of the palace, hid the prophets in a cave during the time of famine and fed them, even though
the king Ahab asked him to help find grass to feed the cattle.

These were the days of Elijah the prophet, who stood alone
as a prophet of Yahweh while the prophets of Baal increased. Elijah
called for a test: bulls would be prepared for sacrifice and each side
would call on their God to provide the fire.

The prophets of Baal called all day but no fire consumed their
offering. Elijah jeered at them and their ineffective god.

Then Elijah set his sacrifice very dramatically, not only pre-

93

paring the bull, but soaking it three times with water. Then he called on God and immediately fire came from heaven, not only consuming the holocaust, but even licking up the water in the trench around the altar.

The people were impressed. Elijah's God had won and all the prophets of Baal were slain.

Ahab went home and told Jezebel his wife about this event and how all Baal's prophets were killed. She swore to kill Elijah and sent him a message telling him so. He fled immediately.

Elijah who showed himself so confident before the 400 and more prophets of Baal now had to flee before a woman. This tells us something about her reputation.

Elijah managed to escape and found new courage.

In spite of his infidelities, Ahab won victories over his enemies. But he never seemed to win any victories over Jezebel.

The story of Naboth and his vineyard shows that plainly.

Naboth had a vineyard next to the palace of Ahab and Ahab wanted it. He offered to buy it or to give him a better one elsewhere.

Naboth would not sell. This was the heritage given to him by his ancestors. Ahab went home gloomy and in bad temper. He lay down and turned his face to the wall, and refused to eat. In a word, he pouted. Jezebel wanted to know what was wrong. He told her and she answered sarcastically, "You make a fine king of Israel, and no mistake! Get up and eat; cheer up, and you will feel better; I will get you the vineyard of Naboth of Jezreel myself."

And she did. She wrote letters accusing Naboth of crimes and had him stoned to death. Then she presented the vineyard to Ahab, which he had no qualms about taking.

That was the last straw. Now Elijah made it clear that Ahab and Jezebel had committed enough crimes. When warned, Ahab repented; Jezebel did not. As promised, she was destroyed and thrown to the dogs.

What are we to make of Jezebel? It seems obvious that Ahab was a weak man who allowed Jezebel to do as she wished, who caved in to every desire of hers.

At other times and under other circumstances, Jezebel could have been a power for good, for she was certainly a power.

Jezebel had the kind of power that is often misplaced.

We have all seen women like Jezebel: she is the power behind the throne. She makes the man do things he would never do on his own and she does it by her jeering at him, nagging him on. She may also do it by her feminine wiles, although we are not told this in connection with Ahab. Only later do we see Jezebel playing the feminine game. With her husband dead, Jehu decided to finish up delayed business, especially with respect to the field of Naboth of Jezreel. Here we see Jezebel getting ready for Jehu's visit by adorning herself and making up her eyes with kohl, the powder women used to darken their eyelids. Perhaps she hoped to win him over even then.

Women, who seldom run countries or businesses or armies or the media, often run their men one on one.

They can do this for evil or for good. Jezebel has become the prototype of those who use their power for evil. Her husband, Ahab, was the prototype of the nagged and henpecked husband. As king of Israel he could govern the whole country, but not his wife, who even led him into idolatry and the killing of prophets.

It has often been said, "Never underestimate the power of a woman." Women do have power. How they use it is another matter.

Discussion:

1. What kinds of power do you think most women have over men?

2. Women of great energy and power often do well in church organizations, but how may they misuse their power?
3. Do you believe there was any antifeminine bias in the way the story of Ahab and Jezebel is told?

FAVORS FOR THE LADIES

Women and Elisha

ELIJAH, THE GREAT PROPHET, WAS TAKEN UP TO HEAVEN IN A chariot and horses of fire. He was gone. His place was taken by Elisha, who had been selected as his successor.

Like his model, Elisha was a wonder worker and that is how he is mostly portrayed.

Many of his wonders involved women. He came to the help of needy women and at times he was brought to others in need by a woman.

One of the first to come to him was a widow, the wife of a member of the prophetic brotherhood. As we know, widows were often in dire straits in Israel. As married women, they had been totally dependent upon their husbands, and now with their source of support gone, they might well find themselves destitute.

Such was the case with this woman. She owed money and when her creditor came and found she had nothing, he wanted to take two children as his slaves.

Elisha immediately offered to help. "What do you have in your house?"

"Nothing," she told him, "except a jar of oil."

He told her to borrow all the jars she could from her neighbor and pour her oil into them. She continued to pour and still had more oil when she ran out of jars. Now she had enough to pay her creditor and plus a little extra to live on.

In such a simple manner, Elisha provided for this poor woman.

Notice that he responded to her need by using what she already had.

This is the image of the poor woman who is not above asking for help, particularly when the lives of her children are at stake.

Another woman, one of rank, we are told, lived in Shunem. She asked Elisha to stop and eat at her house. He did so several times, making it a custom to always break his voyage there when he was traveling in the vicinity.

This woman said to her husband, "Look, I am sure that the man who is constantly passing our way must be a holy man of God. Let us build him a small room on the roof, and put a bed in it, and a table and chair and lamp; whenever he comes to us he can rest there."

And so they did.

Elisha asked her what he could do for her. She asked for nothing. But Elisha asked others and they said that this woman had no son and her husband was old.

Being a widow was one of the fates to be feared in Israel, but so was being sonless. Without a husband, a woman had no one to provide for her. Without a son, she had no one to provide for her in her old age, her widowhood. Nor did she have a way to pass on her life to the next generation.

Elisha called her and told her, "At this time next year, you will hold a son in your arms."

And so it came to pass. The son, the apple of his parents' eyes, was born and grew up. But one day during reaping, the child complained of pain in his head, and within hours he was dead.

His mother, who saw her son as the gift of the prophet Elisha, laid him on the prophet's bed and went for Elisha. He told her to take his staff and stretch it over the child's body. She insisted that he come with her himself.

And so he did, and he raised the child to life.

The situation of this woman of Shunem was different in some ways from that of the poor woman. She was not poor, but she was needy, not having a son. And yet she did not make a single request for herself. It was up to others to ask for her. She is the type of woman who is the do-gooder. She recognized what type of man Elisha was and wanted to provide for him. She wanted to have him as a guest in her house. It was she who went to her husband and suggested the building of the room.

Later, when her son died, it again was not the husband who took the initiative. In fact, we do not even see evidence that the father left the fields. He sent the boy back to the house with a servant.

But his wife, in this case, did not wait for others to make her claim with the prophet. She got a donkey saddled, in spite of the protests of the servant, and set off to get him to come.

He agreed to help her, but he did not offer to come personally. That was not good enough for her. She was not about to take a chance with her son's life. She would not leave him until he came.

He came, and the boy was brought back to life.

This is the strong woman who will do whatever is necessary for her son.

Another incident, the curing of Naaman the leper, came about through the words of the little slave girl who told her master about Elisha, the prophet in Israel. We know nothing more about her, but she was the link that led to the cure.

This third woman, the little slave girl, is simply the person who is in the position to pass along the information that she has. Although she is only a slave, she is listened to, and this is an indication of the respect that attends her. Slaves in those days were often the results of war and conflicts and not necessarily seen as less than human, as has happened in other periods of history.

Three women: one a recipient of charity, one an instigator, and the third in control of the circumstances.

It is rare for women to be miracle-workers in their own right, in the Scriptures or out of it, but they are always there for the miracles, always witnesses, and often the causes.

Discussion:

1. How are the first two women alike, and how are they different?
2. What does it mean to you that most miracles worked were for the sake of males?
3. Which of these women do you think the church today has most of?

LADY WITH THE SCIMITAR

Judith

J UDITH WAS A REMARKABLE WOMAN, UNUSUAL FOR HER TIME or, indeed, for any time. Her name means "Jewess," suggesting an example of what a true Jewish woman should be.

She lived during the time when Nebuchadnezzar was king of the Assyrians and Holofernes was general-in-chief of the armies. Holofernes was the kind of general who was used to winning. His battle plans usually consisted of overtaking people, if not by battle, then by starving them out.

It was the latter method he chose for the Israelites. After a while they were short of food, but more seriously, they were short of water. Every water jar was empty, the wells were drying up, people were fainting from thirst. The chief men of the town, including the leader Uzziah, finally told the people:

"We will hold out for five more days. If God doesn't help us in that amount of time, we will sue for peace."

It is at that point in the story that Judith is introduced. She was a wealthy widow, a woman of great renown and beauty. When she heard what was being said, she upbraided the leaders for putting God to the test. What right did they have to put a time limit on God?

101

Uzziah replied that she was right, but he didn't know what to do to help the people. Judith said not to worry, she would take care of things.

After spending some time in very serious prayer, she dressed in her finest and with a maid, set out for the Assyrian camp. Everyone was immediately impressed with her beauty and daring. Not only did they allow her to pass, but they escorted her directly to Holofernes. He too was much impressed and listened as she explained that as soon as the Israelites disobeyed God's law they would easily be routed.

By the third day Judith was ready to do what she had come to do. She was invited to a banquet by Holofernes and sat at his own table. He had hoped to seduce her and even feared that if he let the opportunity pass with a woman like her, he would be laughed at by the nations.

They ate and drank, and Holofernes continued to drink. At last he fell drunk upon his bed. This was the moment Judith was waiting for. She took Holofernes' own scimitar and cut off his head and carried it back to her people.

This daring deed was just what the Israelites needed to give them new courage and new hope and just what was needed to destroy the morale of the Assyrians.

The Israelites were saved, Judith was honored, and they all lived happily ever after.

Some people who read this story are shocked at the bloody deed of such a beautiful lady. Others are disappointed that it is yet another case of a woman who used her beauty and feminine wiles to overcome a man. But Judith was totally admirable in her devotion to God and her people. She was a strong woman, completely in control of herself and those around her.

What about the use of those feminine wiles? Is that perhaps why women have them? Women cannot usually fight the way men do, with strength of arms. But they can outwit men, who are often, like Holofernes, overcome with their desire for the women.

It is interesting that Holofernes drank too much that night. Surely, one would say, he knew better. But perhaps he realized that Judith was no ordinary woman, certainly not like one of his own women who would be all too eager to fall into his arms. No, here was a woman that he needed to impress. And he drank to keep up his courage.

People who are put off by the bloodiness of cutting off Holofernes' head must try to suggest another way she could have achieved what she set out to do. Seeing the lifeless and headless body of Holofernes had the desired effect on the Assyrians. Hanging the head on the walls had the desired effect on the Israelites. And the fact that it took a woman to achieve what the men could not do had another effect. We are told in the story that the women danced along with Judith at the end. They recognized her as one of their own.

It should be added that according to many biblical scholars, this story is not an historical event, but rather a story teaching a lesson. The lesson is simply that the Jews, no matter what happens, should trust God. God saves his people by the deeds of men, acting as men (or women). And the rise and fall of the people of God is likely to be dependent on their fidelity to the law.

Discussion:

1. For whom would Judith be a heroine? For soldiers? For women fighters?
2. What are the admirable traits of Judith that modern women could emulate?
3. Do you see Judith as the model of Jewish women, or any women, as the writer of this story apparently did?

SAVED BY A WOMAN

Esther

KING AHASUERUS WAS A DESPOT, THE IMAGE OF THE ORIEN-
tal ruler who held both his empire and the lives of his
people in his hands. He was also apparently easily angered
and easily influenced. Like a figure out of the Arabian Nights he
held sumptuous banquets and frequent celebrations. According
to 1:4, one of his celebrations went on for a hundred and eighty
days, about half a year!

The queen's name was Vashti and while the king was celebrating with the men, she was celebrating equally with the
women. The king wanted to show her off, her beauty adorned with
gorgeous clothes and jewels. Vashti refused to come.

Her reason is not given. Perhaps she was simply tired, but
more than likely she did not wish to be displayed like an object to
the men.

Ahasuerus was not accustomed to being disobeyed and he
was very angry that Vashti should simply refuse to come. He consulted his wise men as to what should be done. Their answer was
amazing: "Vashti has wronged not only the king, but also all the
administrators and nations inhabiting the provinces of King

Ahasuerus. The queen's conduct will soon become known to all the women and encourage them in a contemptuous attitude toward their husbands, since they will say, 'King Ahasuerus ordered Queen Vashti to appear before him and she did not come.' The wives of all the Persian and Median administrators will hear of the queen's answer before the day is out, and will start talking to the king's administrators in the same way; that will mean contempt and anger all around."

How dangerous it is to allow women to express themselves! One woman refusing to allow herself to be treated as an object and the whole kingdom will come tumbling down!

Their decision was that Vashti was never to appear again before the king, nor may any woman do so, unless called. All men would be masters in their own homes!

But now the king was without a queen, so in the manner of Oriental potentates, a number of beautiful women were selected for him. Among them was Esther, an orphan adopted by Mordecai, a Jew.

The young women were prepared at length for their duties to the king, an entire year being devoted to this. Further they had fine rooms and fine food and servants to attend them. And all this for the privilege of spending one night with him, or more if he was especially pleased with them.

Esther pleased him the most and he decided to make her his queen.

Now the plot thickens. The star of the power-hungry Haman was rising and since Mordecai refused to bow before him, he determined to get rid of both Mordecai and all the Jews. He received the power from the king to destroy all these people, these "unassimilated" people, as he called them.

This was an early pogrom, one whose pattern would sadly be copied throughout the centuries.

But Mordecai learned what was to happen and soon so did

Esther. She also knew that she would not be exempted from the destruction just because she lived in the king's palace. But, as Mordecai told her, perhaps she was in the palace just so she could do something for her people.

She encouraged her people and she herself spent a long time in prayer, as do others in the Scriptures when they set out on dangerous missions.

After three days of prayer, she dressed in her best and went to see the king. When he saw her, he was angry at first, but then, as the story tells us, God changed his heart. He asked her what she wanted and she said she would tell him the next day at a banquet to which Haman was also to be invited.

The whole story comes out at the banquet and Haman's fate is sealed. His end comes quickly; he is hanged on the gallows he had erected for Mordecai and the people are saved. Not only that but they are allowed and encouraged to avenge themselves on their enemies and two days of slaughter ensue, with thousands of people killed.

Scripture scholar John McKenzie indicates a number of problems with this story: it is likely non-historical and in the Hebrew text God is not even mentioned (the Greek text contains additional material, including prayers and references to God). Further, some persons are put off by the bloody revenge that the Jews took against their enemies.

But none of those are the message of this book. Rather, the providence of God is highlighted, the concept that he will look after his own. He looks after his own through people, in this case, Esther, who, it seems, was raised to the position of queen just for this purpose.

Like several other of the Old Testament women, Esther is portrayed as unusually attractive and she used her attractiveness as well as her feminine wiles to achieve what she desired. For example the Scriptures mention that when she went to see the king, she was weak with fasting, but we are told: "With a delicate air she leaned on one (maid), while the other accompanied her carrying her train. She leaned on the maid's arm as though languidly, but in fact because her body was too weak to support her.... Rosy with the full flush of her beauty, her face radiated joy and love: but her heart shrank with fear."

She had good reason to be afraid. If she failed to win over the king, he would put her to death for appearing in his presence. The only way she could accomplish her desire was to play on his love of her.

Esther is sometimes used as a prototype of Mary, under the title of the Immaculate Conception. The laws that were made for others were not for her. She was exempt.

Discussion:

1. Does this story show the power of women? Is women's power always so different from men's power?
2. Do you see Esther as passive and unduly under the influence of Mordecai?
3. When women have the opportunity, are they always as bloodthirsty as Esther seems to be or does history show them as more compassionate?

COMPANION IN MISERY

Job's Wife

W E ALL KNOW JOB. HE WAS THE MAN IN THE STORY WHO served as sort of a pawn in a wager between God and Satan. Beyond that he was the vehicle to attempt an answer in dramatic form to an ancient question: why suffering?

According to the story, Job was accustomed to the good life. He had seven sons and three daughters, exactly what any devout Jew would like to have: several sons to carry on his name and a few daughters to bear him grandchildren. In addition, he had seven thousand sheep, three thousand camels, five hundred yoke of oxen and five hundred she-donkeys: he was enormously rich. To handle all of his property he had many servants.

We are also told that he was very devout. When members of his family held their many banquets he would offer sacrifice the next day to make amends for any sin, even in their hearts, that his family might have committed.

Such a man would serve as a perfect test. Did he love God because he had all these possessions? Would he still love God without them?

The test was given. He lost everything. Later, he even lost

his health and was reduced to sitting in an ash pit and scraping his wounds with a piece of a broken pot. Job did not lose faith.

However, his wife came to talk to him. Her words were quite harsh: "Do you now still mean to persist in your blamelessness? Curse God and die."

Job replied, "That is how foolish women talk. If we take happiness from God's hand, must we not take sorrow too?"

That is the only time we hear anything from Job's wife. It is not the last we hear from Job.

But Job passes the test, although he does not yet find a satisfactory answer to the meaning of pain. Nor will he, nor will we.

Of course this is only a story, and neither Job nor his wife were real people, nor did God and Satan ever discuss a human being and bet on how he would act.

Still the story is very instructive. Job is quite an admirable person. When we meet his wife, however, we are left with the impression of a woman not quite worthy of him. She is ready to give up on God.

However, we are forgetting that if Job lost everything, so did she. Gone were her children and the good life she was accustomed to.

Job tells her she is talking like a foolish woman. And perhaps these words fall uneasily on our ears.

Too often men call women foolish and belittle their concerns.

In this story, Job is clearly in the right and his wife in the wrong, but the pattern is very common. The man is called by God to do specific tasks, to right wrongs, to make a commitment, to undertake a work that the woman only minimally understands. But she too is expected to make the sacrifices.

Now the image that many people have of women is that they are more emotional, dreamier, and more romantic than men. How often, however, the exact opposite is the case. It is the woman who is the realist. The man wants to conquer the world; the woman wonders what she will serve for dinner tonight. The man wants to take the big risk and invest in something that may make him rich or make him destitute; the woman is concerned with a safe and secure home for the children.

One often wonders how it was for the wife of Moses who had to take the big risks, or the wife of Peter when Peter left all and followed the Master, or even the wife of Pilate. The men were called or made their decisions, but the women also had to pay the price.

Job survived his test. We do not know whether his wife did. We do know that in the end, Job was rewarded.

Instead of seven thousand sheep, he now had fourteen thousand sheep. Instead of five hundred camels, he now had a thousand camels, and so on. He received double of everything.

He even had new sons and daughters, although not double. We do not know if this meant that his wife now gave birth to ten more children, or if he also got a new wife in the bargain.

But there is an interesting development with his new children: "He had seven sons and three daughters; his first daughter he called 'Turtledove,' the second 'Cassia,' and the third 'Mascara.' Throughout the land there were no women as beautiful as the daughters of Job. And their father gave them inheritance rights like their brothers."

Notice that not even one of his seven sons is mentioned by name or by attribute. It was his daughters who apparently filled him with joy and they received inheritance rights like their brothers. Quite a change from the usual procedure.

Perhaps Job learned something in his misfortunes. Perhaps he learned that in his miseries, he missed his women. We do not know how much support his wife gave him, after that initial conversation. His friends, however, in spite of their long discourses, were of little comfort. Perhaps he missed his sweet daughters and learned not to take his new daughters for granted.

Discussion:

1. How do you picture Job's wife?
2. What do you make of the final passage of this story with the emphasis on his new daughters?
3. Give modern examples of when man is the dreamer and the woman must also pay for the dreams.

THE STRONG WOMAN

Poem of the Perfect Wife

T HIS IS THAT OFTEN-QUOTED PASSAGE ABOUT THE PERFECT wife. It is an open question whether when women hear this read, they agree with it and are led to emulate this woman's qualities or are totally put off by it.

Let us take a look at it, noting first of all that it describes a perfect wife, not a perfect woman.

"A perfect wife — who can find her?"

Does this mean that such perfection is rare? No doubt it does, but, of course, any kind of perfection is rare. In any case, it is nice to know that her price is far beyond the price of pearls!

The perfect wife is the one who pleases her husband. And how does she do this?

She does it with her diligent work: "She is always busy with wool and with flax, she does her work with eager hands."

She gets up early, and gets the household working; she is a business woman, too, buying fields and planting vineyards. She also weaves linen sheets and sells them.

The perfect wife is pictured as being a woman with strong arms, developed during her years of hard work. Not only does she run her household, but she herself leads in the work, both with her "feminine" skills with a needle and whatever else needs to be done.

She is generous with the needy, but her own family is always well-cared for.

Because of her, her husband is highly respected. When she speaks it is to offer wise counsel. With her everything is well run and there is no idle word or idle body. Her sons and her husband praise her.

The passage concludes with the words: "Charm is deceitful, and beauty empty; the woman who is wise is the one to praise!"

And a final comment: "Give her a share in what her hands have worked for, and let her works tell her praises at the city gates."

There was perhaps a time when this passage spoke to women, but today's American women are unlikely to be impressed by it.

The woman gets up early and works hard all day, so that her husband can be respected. She will be praised by her menfolk, and she is to be given a share in what her work has accomplished. How nice, some women would say.

Women today will say that this passage illustrates a different world, one in which women were second class people, whose job it was to serve. (Jesus said that he had come to serve and not be served, and thus set an example for all men.) In that world, no one would have talked about women fulfilling their potential or women having any rights of their own, or of men doing things that would help women use their talents.

That is perhaps why this passage is more or less shrugged off by women today.

It is also significant that that line, "Charm is deceitful and beauty empty; the woman who is wise is the one to praise!" is included.

However, in the Bible itself, rarely is this axiom acted upon. Again and again we see men attracted by the beauty of and honoring such women, even making great sacrifices for them.

It is only the older man, perhaps, who can appreciate the wisdom of a woman.

But a closer second look shows that perhaps this passage speaks more today than ever. Here the woman is praised for her work. If she does needlework and weaving, if she plants vineyards, she is doing what would have been done in her time. Today perhaps we would say that she opens her own business or goes into a profession.

Still today it is good and honorable for a woman to provide well for her family; no other success can take the place of failure there. Also the perfect wife is still the one who looks out for the needy; this is a proud heritage of women.

And finally there is nothing at all wrong about doing what is necessary to build up the men in one's life. Any woman who loves her husband and her son wants to do that. And many women have learned how they can combine their support for their families with their own self-development. It is not easy, but that is why the perfect wife is strong.

Discussion:

1. How would you picture the perfect wife?
2. How would you picture the perfect husband?
3. Do you think that, except physically, most women are stronger than their men?

The Song of Songs

WORLD'S GREATEST LOVE SONG

Song of Solomon

T HIS IS THE POEM THAT CONTINUES TO INSPIRE AND TO SHOCK. Some persons have never read it and others who read it claim that it can only be understood allegorically. In *The Dictionary of the Bible,* John McKenzie states that besides the literal meaning of the passages, there is even more erotic symbolism than appears under the surface.

With that in mind, some simply avoid reading this, as if eroticism is not quite appropriate for a divinely inspired book.

Even though today some of the expressions of love in the book are either obscure or distasteful to us, the book itself, it seems, tells us that eroticism too is of God.

Those who find difficulties with the book often seem to be giving vent to the following problems:

1. Should so much love be given to a woman? One's whole heart and soul and mind and body should be devoted to God.
2. Even if human love is sanctified, should it be so total and so obviously enjoyed? Should not one exercise a little more control?

Notice how both of these questions concern the idea that has been a problem for Christianity through the ages in one way or another. What is the place of sex? Is it simply another one of God's great gifts, or is it a necessary evil?

There have been times in the history of the Church when the latter was emphasized. St. Augustine, one of the great lights of the Church, even counseled people to try not to enjoy sex. Sex is for the procreation of children, but that was its only redeeming value. He thought that sex, even in marriage, was at least a venial sin.

Others have taken a less extreme approach, but the image of a more perfect life has often included the total renunciation of sex. This has been particularly true for women. A list of the canonized women saints of the Catholic Church will show that most of them were either virgins or martyrs or virgin-martyrs.

The distaste for sex, the attitude that all sex is somehow "dirty" is not just a Puritan idea. It often is a reaction against the overindulgence in sex that is rampant in worldly lives. Everyone knows that adultery can destroy relationships not only between a husband and wife, but also for the children. Rape is a particularly despicable crime since it uses sex as a form of violence and a destruction of this most precious gift.

For sex and all its uses are very precious. The giving of oneself to another human being can and should be a very profound human act. As such, it should be a delight for both partners, both physically and emotionally.

The Song of Songs points up these aspects strongly.

How beautiful some of the lines are:

The bride speaks:

"My Beloved is mine and I am his."
"I found him whom my heart loves. I held him fast,
  nor would I let him go."

The groom speaks:

"You ravish my heart, my sister, my promised bride, you ravish my heart with a single one of your glances, with one single pearl of your necklace. What spells lie in your love, my sister, my promised bride!"

These are the lines that anyone who has ever been in love can identify with. These are the lines that speak strongly of human love.

Human love was created by God to give joy to human beings. It is not possible that something that is given by God to human beings can be considered unworthy.

The most powerful and the best way that human love can be expressed is through sex, and sex can be enormously pleasurable, probably the highest pleasure that can be experienced. Perhaps our culture, which so indulges sex on every level and degrades it too, still has a long way to go to see sex as beautiful and sanctifying.

Discussion:

1. Why do you think that so many people who appreciate God's other gifts tend to deny this one?
2. What do you think is happening today with eroticism in the popular media?
3. Select your favorite lines from this poem and compare them.

A WOMAN ACCUSED

Susanna

THE STORY OF SUSANNA HAS BEEN CALLED THE WORLD'S FIRST detective story. It is easy to imagine this story presented as a television show. We see the beautiful Susanna walking in the garden in the afternoon. We see the old men, judges with lust in their hearts, hiding behind the trees.

Susanna decides that this would be a good day to bathe in the garden pool. She sends her maids to fetch the oil and balsam and to close the garden gates.

Now the old men come forward and tell her that if she refuses them, they will accuse her of being with a young man.

Susanna sighs, "I am trapped," she says, "whatever I do. If I agree, that means my death; if I resist, I cannot get away from you. But I prefer to fall innocent into your power than to sin in the eyes of God."

She calls loudly, as do the old judges, and everyone comes running, fearing the worst. True to their word, the old judges give their story of what happened.

The people are astonished. Susanna had the reputation of walking in the law of the Lord.

The trial is held. Susanna comes heavily veiled, surrounded by her whole family. She is made to remove the veil, so, once again, the men can feast on her beauty. The old judges are believed; they are highly respected and feared because every day they make judgments about others.

And Susanna is led away to be executed.

Then Daniel, a young boy, raises his voice: "I am innocent of the death of this woman."

Everyone stares at him. What could he mean? And then, in a most simple way, he traps the old men through their own words.

Daniel is very sure of himself. As he asks the old judges the question about which tree in the garden, he first insults them. A very bold procedure to take with men who have the power to condemn!

Daniel is the hero of this story, but Susanna is a heroine. She is seen as not only very beautiful, but also very rich, from a good family, and married to a highly respected man. Above all, she lives a life that is above reproach.

Yet the people are willing, just like that, to condemn her on the word of the two judges.

Not only can this story be called the first detective story, but it is an early story of sexual harassment. And it is an extreme case. Susanna is only one of the many women through the ages who have had to make the decision to either compromise themselves or to lose their jobs, their positions, their promotions, or their reputations.

Susanna was fortunate to have Daniel. Many women today are also so fortunate. But others have found that they will need to fight the battles themselves. Even today, the odds are stacked against them, although less than they once were. Susanna, even with the support of all her relatives, was about to be executed. She was a victim and there was little she could do for herself. Today there is much that any woman can do.

Women today do not necessarily need to be victims if they do not want to be. They can take control of their own lives. They can band together to support and help each other. But more importantly, they can try to help establish relationships with men that are less rocky.

Contacts and relationships between the sexes are never easy. Men and women often do not even seem to be speaking the same language. Men and women are often much attracted to each other, but at the same time, they find each other incomprehensible. Even in a good marriage that has endured for many years, there are often misunderstandings.

Susanna's case, however, was not one of misunderstanding. It was very clear to Susanna exactly what the judges meant to do, and Susanna made it very clear that she could not acquiesce. In her case it was one of power which often is what it is all about. As long as women stay in positions where they cannot challenge men's power, many men feel satisfied. Problems arise when men feel threatened.

Further, as is well known, rape is less a sex crime than it is a crime of violence. As such, it too is a matter of power.

Power plays come from people who are insecure. Do we have more such crimes today because we have more insecure people? It would be interesting to examine this question.

Discussion:

1. Can you draw any parallels between what happened between Susanna and the judges and what is happening in offices and businesses these days?
2. Women are often accused of "asking for it." Could Susanna have done anything differently?
3. Would there be less sexual harassment if women all stayed at home with their children?

LOVE AND BETRAYAL

Gomer, Wife of Hosea

WHAT A STRANGE AND SAD STORY! HOSEA IS TOLD TO marry a prostitute, who gives him three children, all with unusual names to say the least, and then apparently leaves him.

Later he marries her again.

The comparison of marrying a prostitute to the unfaithfulness of Israel to God is vividly portrayed.

And yet, according to many Scripture scholars, this is not merely an allegorical story. Hosea really did marry a prostitute, although we do not know whether he knew that was her situation before he married her.

The nation of Israel, like so many people before and after, has often been unfaithful to their God, and the comparison is a powerful one.

But let us look at the unfaithful wife, not merely an adulteress, but even, in this case, one who gives herself for money.

Throughout Scripture, the prostitute is often pictured as the ultimate in bad women. Even today, this is generally true. There are people who imagine that being a prostitute is the worst thing a woman can do.

On the other side of the coin, many movies and television stories today show prostitution in a glamorous light. The prostitute is the absolutely gorgeous woman who is both wise and wily and men pay dearly, but willingly, for her services.

Neither of these images are quite accurate. It would be hard to say that prostitution is the worst sin for a woman, considering how often a woman is forced into thinking that she has no other way to make a living. In such cases, can prostitution be as evil as the social circumstances that deprive her of a livelihood? Or can prostitution compare with hatred and harming of other human beings? Further, is the prostitute more a sinner than the client who uses her services, who is not in any way forced to do so?

Or again, although there are no doubt glamorous women prostituting themselves, it can hardly be considered a glamorous life. Every client can be a danger of AIDS or other diseases and none of them see her as a whole person, but merely as a commodity. Even if she earns a great deal of money, the working years will be short and full of danger. Typical clients are always looking for younger and younger women.

Prostitution is very ancient and has been called the oldest profession. Through the centuries it has often been frowned upon, but rarely removed completely from any city or country. Even in countries where there is no moral prohibition against it, it has the effect of dehumanization on a young woman. One cannot see oneself as an object without a loss of personhood.

The other word used for this wife of Hosea is that of adulteress. Adultery, quite another thing from prostitution, is roundly condemned in both Testaments, particularly and sometimes only when it is committed by a woman. She is giving to another man what she owes to her husband.

As long as only wives are punished for adultery and husbands are not, then here too women are seen as commodities, as objects belonging to their husbands. As such, this attitude has the same dehumanizing effect.

Gomer, Hosea's wife, does not seem to have been forced into prostitution or adultery. We do not know what motivated her, but we can imagine that the dehumanizing effect made her an unhappy woman. Perhaps she, like many such women, could not ever quite believe that even when she was married, her husband loved her for herself. Persons who feel they are not loved continue to seek love, often in all the wrong places. They believe that if they attract enough lovers that perhaps quantity will replace quality. It never works; the end result is only a deeper sense of loss of self.

Some women today have attempted to cut themselves loose, so to speak, from the restrictions of the past, and to use sex as readily and promiscuously as some men have done.

They believe that in so doing they will be liberated. They find instead that they have lost much more than they have gained.

Another thought of this story, though, is of great consolation. God loves human beings so much that even when they are unfaithful, when they have committed every kind of crime and sin, he is willing to take them back. Human beings are precious to him.

Discussion:

1. Do you think that even today there is too much emphasis placed on prostitutes as evil temptresses?
2. Persons who are unfaithful to each other in a marriage tend to blame their partners for not satisfying their needs. Respond to this.
3. Do you find yourself feeling somewhat sorry for Gomer? Why?

MOTHER OF MARTYRS

Mother of the Seven Maccabee Brothers

T HE STORY OF THE SEVEN BROTHERS IS TOLD WITH ESPECIALLY vivid detail. They were arrested with their mother and the king tried to force them to taste pig's flesh. They completely refused and they were routinely beaten.

One of them acted as spokesman and told the king boldly that they would rather die than disobey the laws of their ancestors.

The king was furious and ordered for him horrible tortures: He was to be torn apart and fried in a red hot pan. As the execution was carried out, his mother and brothers were there watching his painful death.

They encouraged him with promises of God's watchfulness and his pity.

After his death, the second son was killed in the same manner. And so on with the other sons. Each one seemed to act bolder and more courageously.

The mother watched the entire time and always encouraged her sons. The Scriptures remark: "But the mother was especially admirable and worthy of honorable remembrance, for she watched the death of seven sons in the course of a single day, and endured it resolutely because of her hopes in the Lord. Indeed she encouraged each of them in the language of their ancestors; filled with noble conviction, she reinforced her womanly argument with manly courage, saying to them, 'I do not know how you appeared in my womb; it was not I who endowed you with breath and life, I had not the shaping of your every part. It is the creator of the world, ordaining the process of man's birth and presiding over the origin of all things, who in his mercy will most surely give you back both breath and life, seeing that you now despise your own existence for the sake of his laws.'"

Then they came to the youngest son, the one most mothers dote on, the one who will be their last best hope. The king, Antiochus, appealed to him and promised under oath to make him rich and happy if he would abandon his traditions. He would become a Friend of the Court and be entrusted with public office.

The young man paid no attention, so the king turned to the mother. "Why don't you encourage him," he said, "this is your last son. Don't you want him to live?"

Finally the mother agreed to talk to this son. When she did, she spoke in her own language to her son and the king did not understand. What she told him was very different from what the king expected.

She told him, out of pity for her to be courageous like his brothers, so that she could forever be proud of him.

The son took it to heart and denounced the king and died manfully, even though his death was the most cruel. And finally, the mother too was put to death. She was able to join her sons in death and in another life.

Any mother, any woman, reading this story will be impressed with this mother. It is hard enough to lose a son, much less all seven of her sons. It is hard enough to see a son die peacefully in his bed, much less to see him cruelly tortured before your eyes.

It would be the most normal, natural thing in the world for a woman to at least tell her son that she would rather see him alive than anything else.

But this woman steeled herself to the highest point and attained martyrdom along with her sons.

This woman is the model of all women who support and stand behind their men, their sons and their husbands. She is the one who will never ask her men to turn aside from what they believe in, just to protect her, or out of pity for her. She is the model of the woman who is able to rise above her natural instincts to protect her sons.

She was able to do this only because she had faith in God. She knew that this life was not all there was, and that in the next life she would be reunited with her sons.

What a profound mystery we have here. It has often been remarked upon that only faith helps one to endure the miseries and sorrows of life, including the greatest sorrow of all, the death of loved ones. Only if we believe that this life is not all, that death is not final, can we endure it.

Without faith, very little in life makes sense. Certainly not the cruelties of nature or the greater cruelties of evil persons.

The mother of the seven Maccabee brothers is not given a name. Her name could be any name, any woman who gives her son. She calls to mind especially Mary standing at the foot of the cross, never asking Jesus to forsake what he is doing for her, even though her heart is breaking.

Some have said that it is man's place to do and die and woman's place to watch and wait and suffer. These roles overlap many times, but there is still some truth in them. It would be hard to say which sufferings are more difficult.

Discussion:

1. Does this woman impress you as cold and heartless, even stoic?
2. Can women whose sons are executed for crimes relate to this woman, although their sons are not dying innocently?
3. What do you make of the idea of woman's role to watch and wait and suffer?

Conclusion

WHAT STRONG WOMEN THESE WOMEN OF THE OLD TEStament were! The roles that many of them were asked to play were difficult and challenging ones, but they were able to rise to the occasion. If they could not win by frontal assault, they won by charm or conniving. These were not plastic saints whose lives bear no resemblance to ours. In spite of the fact that thousands of years separate them from us, they seem as real as our neighbors next door. They are flesh and blood heroines and we respond to them that way, sometimes with sympathy, sometimes with a "bravo!", sometimes with a shaking of our head.

It is because they are so real that they are worth reading about and thinking about. All Scripture, St. Paul tells us, was written for our instruction. There is so much we can learn from these women. No matter whether we are wife or mother or neither; no matter if we are ambitious or retiring, gentle or rambunctious; no matter if we are young and beautiful or old and wrinkled, there is someone in the Old Testament like us.

These women were women of destiny. They tell us that we too are women of destiny, whatever our path of life may be.

Bibliography

Aschliman, Sylvia Albrecht, "A New Look at Women of Old," *The Bible Today*, Vol. 28, No. 6, Nov., 1990, pp. 353-357.

Bergant, Dianne, C.S.A., *Introduction to the Bible*. Collegeville Bible Commentary. Collegeville, MN: Liturgical Press, 1985.

Craghan, John F., *Exodus*. Collegeville Bible Commentary. Collegeville, MN: Liturgical Press, 1985.

Fischer, James A., C.M., *God Said: Let There Be Woman*. New York: Alba House, 1979.

Hoppe, Leslie J., O.F.M., "The Bible on Women," *The Bible Today*, Vol. 28, No. 6, Nov., 1990, pp. 330-335.

Keller, Werner, *The Bible as History*. New York: Morrow, 1981.

Kirk, Martha Ann, C.C.V.I., *God of our Mothers: Seven Biblical Women Tell Their Stories* (set of 2 tapes). Cincinnati: St. Anthony Messenger, 1985.

Maher, Michael, M.S.C., *Genesis*. Wilmington, DE: Michael Glazier, 1982.

Mainelli, Helen Kenik, *Numbers*. Collegeville Bible Commentary. Collegeville, MN: Liturgical Press, 1985.

McKenzie, John L., *Dictionary of the Bible*. New York: Macmillan, 1965.

Nowell, Irene, O.S.B., "Roles of Women in the Old Testament," *The Bible Today*. Vol. 28, No. 6, Nov., 1990, pp. 364-368.

Stuhlmueller, Carroll, C.P., "The Women of Genesis," *The Bible Today*. Vol. 28, No. 6, Nov., 1990, pp. 347-352.

Vawter, Bruce, C.M., *Amos, Hosea, Micah, With an Introduction to Classical Prophecy*. Wilmington, DE: Michael Glazier, 1981.

Viviano, Pauline A., *Genesis*. Collegeville Bible Commentary. Collegeville, MN: Liturgical Press, 1985.